KEITH JARRETT'S
THE KÖLN CONCERT

OXFORD STUDIES IN RECORDED JAZZ

Series Editor   JEREMY BARHAM

KEITH JARRETT'S
THE KÖLN CONCERT

PETER ELSDON

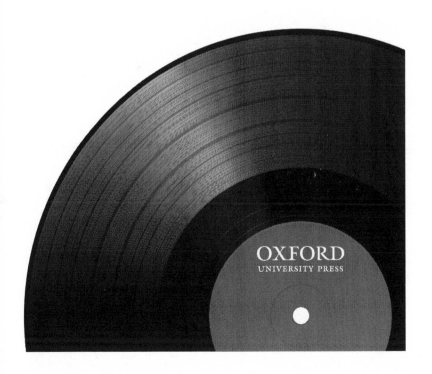

OXFORD
UNIVERSITY PRESS

Oxford University Press is a department of the
University of Oxford. It furthers the University's objective
of excellence in research, scholarship, and education
by publishing worldwide.

Oxford   New York
Auckland   Cape Town   Dar es Salaam   Hong Kong   Karachi
Kuala Lumpur   Madrid   Melbourne   Mexico City   Nairobi
New Delhi   Shanghai   Taipei   Toronto

With offices in
Argentina   Austria   Brazil   Chile   Czech Republic   France   Greece
Guatemala   Hungary   Italy   Japan   Poland   Portugal   Singapore
South Korea   Switzerland   Thailand   Turkey   Ukraine   Vietnam

Oxford is a registered trademark of Oxford University Press
in the UK and certain other countries.

Published in the United States of America by
Oxford University Press
198 Madison Avenue, New York, NY 10016

Library of Congress Cataloging-in-Publication Data
Elsdon, Peter.
Keith Jarrett's the Köln concert / Peter Elsdon.
p. cm.—(Oxford studies in recorded jazz)
Includes bibliographical references and index.
Discography: p.
ISBN 978-0-19-977925-3 (alk. paper)—ISBN 978-0-19-977926-0 (alk. paper)
1. Jarrett, Keith—Performances—Germany—Cologne.
2. Jazz—History and criticism.   I. Title.
ML417.J35E47 2013
786.2'165092—dc23   2012012686

1 3 5 7 9 8 6 4 2
Printed in the United States of America
on acid-free paper

SERIES PREFACE

THE OXFORD STUDIES IN Recorded Jazz series offers detailed historical, cultural, and technical analysis of jazz recordings across a broad spectrum of styles, periods, performing media, and nationalities. Each volume, authored by a leading scholar in the field, addresses either a single jazz album or a set of related recordings by one artist/group, placing the recordings fully in their historical and musical context, and thereby enriching our understanding of their cultural and creative significance.

With access to the latest scholarship and with an innovative and balanced approach to its subject matter, the series offers fresh perspectives on both well-known and neglected jazz repertoire. It sets out to renew musical debate in jazz scholarship, and to develop the subtle critical languages and vocabularies necessary to do full justice to the complex expressive, structural, and cultural dimensions of recorded jazz performance.

JEREMY BARHAM
SERIES EDITOR

CONTENTS

ACKNOWLEDGMENTS

In writing this book, I have been fortunate to benefit from the help and assistance of many individuals. The Faculty of Arts and Social Sciences at the University of Hull funded a semester of study leave in 2010, allowing me time to prepare the manuscript. I am grateful to my colleagues in the Department of Drama and Music, who were willing to help by alleviating some of the pressures of an academic post while I was working on this book.

I would also like to express my thanks to a number of Jarrett enthusiasts. Maurizio Garbolino and Simon Savary both allowed me to share some of their insights on the 1972 and 1975 solo concerts in Europe. Olivier Bruchez, who runs a wonderful website on Jarrett, directed me to various individuals and answered some questions of discography. Tom Gsteiger, Stefan Diller, and Bruno Rub all provided various kinds of assistance. Alyn Shipton was kind enough to provide me with a transcription of his interview with Jarrett for BBC radio, while Marya Burgess at the BBC also helped with some questions. Christopher Chase offered me a copy of his paper on Keith Jarrett and Gurdjieff, and David Nathan at the National Jazz Archive helped me arrange a visit there to locate some print sources. Vera Brandes, who organized the Cologne performance in 1975, helped to put me in touch with various journalists. I owe particular thanks to Hans-Dieter Klinger, for being willing to put aside some time on a holiday to Wales to meet me and talk about his experiences of organizing a Jarrett performance in Germany in January 1975.

I am grateful to Jeremy Barham for the initial impetus to write this book, and for his foresight in establishing this series. At Oxford University Press,

Adam Cohen and Erica Woods Tucker helped with the preparation of the manuscript. The anonymous reviewers who commented both on the proposal for this manuscript and the finished product gave useful suggestions, and they deserve mention here. I am particularly grateful to Stephen Cloud for facilitating the granting of permission for reproduction of excerpts from the published transcription of *The Köln Concert*, and to Keith Jarrett for granting this permission. The excerpts from the transcription used in Chapters Five and Six are used by kind permission of Cavelight Music.

Finally, I must thank my wife, Sarina, who put hours of work into proofreading a draft of the manuscript, and who was willing to put up with the times when I seemed unable to think about anything else; and also to our two cats, Quilly and Marty, whose complete indifference to this project was just the right antidote.

KEITH JARRETT'S
THE KÖLN CONCERT

INTRODUCTION

THE KÖLN CONCERT is undoubtedly pianist Keith Jarrett's most famous record. Widely cited as the best-selling solo piano record of all time following its release in 1975, *The Köln Concert* has now sold somewhere in the region of 3.5 million copies worldwide. Sales figures like this place the record in select company: Miles Davis's *Kind of Blue* (1959), Herbie Hancock's *Headhunters* (1973), and Dave Brubeck's *Time Out* (1959) would be three obvious benchmarks.

This information about the record's sales tells us remarkably little. It merely charts the number of transactions in which the record was purchased and by this measure indicates a release that sold far more than the average for a jazz recording of the time. Such are the markers the music industry prefers as the standard measure of commercial success, but these figures say nothing about who bought this record, why, and how they liked to listen to it. These may not seem obvious questions to ask, given that the music of a record is normally presumed to be the most important determining factor in its popularity. Such were my own inclinations when I first began studying Jarrett's solo improvisations as a doctoral student in the late 1990s. But while I was researching this book, the question of why so many people bought this record came to the forefront of my mind, for a number of reasons. As I was working, two accounts of the record appeared in the mainstream media in the United Kingdom, where I live. Naturally these were of interest, but they also alerted me to a set of ideas about *The Köln Concert* that had to do with much more than just the music. It became clear that these two examples served not only as contemporary markers of opinion but as commentaries on the reception history of the record.

The first was an article that appeared on the website of the Guardian newspaper on January 31, 2011, by John Fordham, which discussed *The Köln Concert* as part of a series entitled "50 Great Moments in Jazz." Fordham identified a series of events, some marked by specific recordings and others much more general in nature.[1] That *The Köln Concert* should appear in this list may be indicative of its place in some kind of historical narrative or canon. But the narrative presented by Fordham is far from being a conventional jazz history. It is a series of disjointed snapshots, perhaps designed to subvert the idea of history as a linear narrative. The Jarrett record fits here not because of its place in a larger historical narrative, but because it is seen as a singular one-off event, a moment in time. As Fordham explains: "From the mid-70s on, [Jarrett's] concerts began to resemble religious rituals, attended by flocks of devotees for whom his music had a meditative, spiritual and transformative power. And all this stemmed from the recording of a single album—conceived as a live concert by a sleep-deprived Jarrett on a faulty grand piano—made in Köln, Germany, on 24 January 1975."[2] Fordham identifies one of the central tensions in contemporary reception of the Cologne recording, namely the way it is sometimes seen to skirt territory described by the pejorative term "easy listening." This is a topic I will return to much later on. But Fordham also ascribes considerable significance to *The Köln Concert* as the source of a powerful and complex idea about Jarrett's music. How can it be that one record should have had such an effect?

The second contemporary treatment of the Cologne concert is more substantial: a documentary broadcast by BBC Radio in April 2011. This program was part of a series entitled "For One Night Only," dealing with live recordings. In the case of the series in question the other albums considered are by Bob Newhart, B. B. King, and Sir Colin Davis with the London Symphony Orchestra. The program opens with an introductory monologue: "Fourteen hundred paying customers, one piano player, no score. This is not the calculus for a successful concert.... The twenty-nine-year-old American jazz pianist Keith Jarrett walked on to the stage of the opera house on his own, sat down at a second-rate piano, and began to play...what's most remarkable is that throughout the whole concert, which lasted over an hour, Keith Jarrett was improvising."[3]

In this case the program plays very heavily on something only alluded to in the *Guardian* article, the fact that this is a recording of a live concert. In the context of a series of broadcasts about live recordings this is hardly surprising, but the program goes on to emphasize the importance of the performance to listeners who were there at the time, who recall hearing "magic" from the very first notes, and witnessing an "unforgettable" performance. What is underlined here is the singularity of the moment, coupled with reminiscences voiced by those who were there at the special moment of the music's creation. These interpretations are prompted not just by the music the audience heard but by one crucial fact that is played upon at the outset of "For One Night Only": that Jarrett's performance was improvised.

The idea of the Cologne concert as a singular unrepeatable moment relies on the intersection of a cultural conception of improvisation as the domain of the ephemeral with the idea of the live recording as opening a window onto the creative moment. So it is that the recording functions to capture a moment that would otherwise have been lost to history, at best the subject of anecdote. This is a view that has come to define the reception of this record, as we will see. And if we are to look for reasons why it should have sold so many copies, and specifically why in America during the latter part of the 1970s it should have been so important, then this needs to be borne in mind.

The other significant fact about the Cologne performance, emphasized particularly in the BBC Radio program, has to do with the circumstances behind the concert and recording. One account has been given repeatedly by Jarrett in interviews, and although it is backed up by accounts from the concert promoter Vera Brandes, and Jarrett's producer and tour manager Manfred Eicher, it is worth repeating here, if only in abbreviated form. On the January 24, 1975, the twenty-nine-year-old American pianist and Eicher arrived in the German city of Cologne, in the midst of a solo European tour. Jarrett was well known to German jazz fans, having toured Europe when he played with saxophonist Charles Lloyd, later with his own trio and quartet, and also with the Miles Davis group. His previous solo piano releases, *Facing You* and *Solo Concerts*, had both been recorded in Europe for Eicher's ECM label. I will explore

Jarrett's critical reception in both Europe and America further in Chapter One, save to say for now that he was well enough regarded to have sold out the Cologne Opera House where he was booked to play (as we will see later on, he had sold out other venues on the same tour).

Rather than flying from Switzerland (Jarrett had performed in Lausanne the previous evening), the two arrived in Eicher's small Volkswagen. Brandes has recalled how she supplied an air ticket from Zurich airport, but for some reason Jarrett chose to cash it in. If Jarrett and Eicher had traveled via Zurich airport, the trip would have been more than 500 miles (800 kilometers). Jarrett's practice was to perform every other day while on tour, in order to allow time for traveling, but in this instance the date that the Cologne Opera House was available meant he had to travel after the Lausanne performance in order to play in Cologne the next night.

Once Jarrett arrived at the venue, he immediately discovered a problem with the Bösendorfer piano.[4] There were some keys that did not release properly when used, the pedal was deficient, and the overall tonal balance of the instrument was unsatisfactory. At this time, Jarrett's contract specified a full-size grand piano in good condition, to be tuned on the day of the performance. Later on, his rider would become much more specific about the models of pianos he would perform on. According to Brandes, the wrong Bösendorfer had been put on the stage of the Opera House, and there was no way to move in the intended instrument within the time available. The efforts of a local piano tuner helped to bring the instrument closer to some kind of playable condition. Jarrett was extremely tired, having by his own account not slept for two days. Even so, partly as the result of considerable persistence and determination on Brandes's part, Jarrett agreed to perform. His own account of the performance includes eating bad Italian food in a restaurant before playing, rushing to finish his meal, almost sending the recording engineers home, and then joking with them before going onstage in an attempt to stay awake. After the performance Brandes recalls running backstage to engineer Martin Wieland to ask: "Did you get that? Did the recording work?"[5] Considering the concert as an event beset by obstacles and setbacks suggests one intriguing idea about this recording: that it should never have happened.

It is appropriate at this point to explain what this book is not about. It is not an attempt to write an account of the making of this recording and the Cologne performance itself. That account already exists, given by the main protagonists in this drama: Jarrett, producer Eicher, and promoter Brandes, along with the voices of audience members. Nor is this book an attempt to document the technical means by which the recording was produced (two Neumann U67 microphones and a Telefunken tape machine, according to Wieland), and the work that went on in the studio to clean it up.[6]

Plenty of books have appeared in recent times about the making of what are sometimes called "iconic" recordings, and this book is not designed to contribute to that genre. Instead, I think of *The Köln Concert* recording as the point at which a number of narratives intersect, and from which they can be traced, forward and backward in time. These strands include the background to Jarrett's solo concert performances, his work both in Europe and America as a musician, the way he came to be seen as a performing musician and improviser, how the recording came to represent something about the creative act, and the manner in which it was appropriated for uses Jarrett did not intend. And then there is, of course, the strand of the music itself: improvised music—created, as Jarrett put it, from nothing, alone on a stage in front of an audience every night. As we will see later, this in itself prompts some questions about how such recorded music might be subject to analytical inquiry, and what analysis might tell us about how Jarrett constructs performances like these. All of these ideas and threads overlap in a variety of ways in this book, placing the recording itself at the center of a complex web. The recording is not the end, but the beginning of inquiry, and even though it is the focus of attention in this book, it is also the starting point for a series of excursions into a variety of theoretical territories.

One of the central themes of this book is the idea, which both the *Guardian* piece and the BBC documentary allude to, of *The Köln Concert* as a special or phenomenal record, not simply because of its sales but because of how listeners have responded to it. I am going to suggest that there was much more involved in this than simply the fact that Jarrett produces a fine performance on record. Rather, it became special because of a kind of ideology, one that can be traced through the cover of the album, other Jarrett recordings and interviews, critical accounts, and in some of the larger cultural themes of the time. *The Köln Concert* came to represent an idea not just about music or art, but about the individual and his or her place in culture.

This is not an idea that is unconnected from the music. I will argue that the music Jarrett created that night in Cologne had the potential to be heard a certain way, against the backdrop of these powerful cultural conceptions. And so a considerable part of this book is, without apology, an examination of the music of the Cologne recording. One of the first parts of this musical survey involves placing the recording in a context that involves Jarrett's other activities and performances around the time, and the jazz scenes, both in Europe and in America, of which he was a part. The musicologist or critic studying a studio recording is inevitably interested in the outtakes; the performances made in the studio that were not released, either not considered good enough or discarded in favor of superior alternatives. The Cologne concert has no outtakes, of course, but what we do have is a lot of other material, which I suggest functions in the same way in that it sits in a dialogic relationship with other performances.

THEORIZING THE LIVE RECORDING

Recordings have played an enormously important role in the dissemination, the development, and even the whole idea of jazz. They have offered the means by which a music created in the heat of live performance could be preserved, documented, and made repeatable. Recordings allow listeners to engage with musical performances, even when geographically and chronologically distant. The point at which the first jazz recording emerges in the twentieth century, the 1917 recording by the Original Dixieland Jazz Band of "Livery Stable Blues," is in many senses the beginning of jazz; it is the first point at which we can hear what the music actually sounded like. All the documentary evidence that comes before can seem subservient, no more than second best to the "real thing." And the writing of jazz history, in its early phases at least, was unthinkable without the existence of recordings. Recordings came to function as a kind of history in themselves.[7]

This very optimistic and even idealistic view of recordings has been challenged in recent times. After all, what a recording reveals is limited, because the very process is illusory. Take Evan Eisenberg, writing in what can justly be called a seminal book on the subject, *The Recording Angel:* "The word record is misleading. Only live recordings record an event; studio recordings, which are the great majority, record nothing."[8] Eisenberg's argument concentrates on how recording creates the illusion that the listener has immediate access to a performance. But even as he seems to mark out a special place for live recordings, he is clear that the notion of fidelity to the original event is a difficult one. Writers dealing with rock and popular music have long recognized that what goes on in the recording studio is increasingly distant from conventional ideas of performance.[9] The recording studio offers the possibility of creating unreal performances. With the techniques of overdubbing and editing available to musicians—techniques that have now been established for decades—

the recorded performance is not necessarily a real performance at all, as musicologist Matthew Butterfield has pointed out in respect of jazz.[10] The use of the recording studio as a creative medium, not simply a tool for capturing a performance, happened first of all in rock music, and it was arguably not fully embraced in jazz until at least the end of the 1960s, when a series of Miles Davis releases involved producer Teo Macero cutting up lengthy studio jams in order to create structured pieces.[11]

Jarrett's *The Köln Concert* belongs to a particular category of jazz recordings, namely those of live records. Eisenberg's comments suggest that some of the same objections may not apply, or rather that such a record may be more faithful to the idea of a live performance than a studio recording might have been. But there are important caveats. A live performance is still subject to treatment in a recording studio, which might include editing and various forms of processing to clean up the sound. Indeed, we know that *The Köln Concert* recording was worked on in the studio before release, mainly because of the below-par piano sound. The consequence is simple but important: our auditory experience listening to Jarrett's recording is not the same as the experience of the audience in that Cologne concert hall, or even the same as Jarrett's experience. Yet part of the cachet of the live recording is the temptation to think that this is so, that we are able to participate in the performance as if audience members. This illusion can be countered by the observation that recorded live performances are still subject to the same technological mediations as studio performances. Butterfield has suggested that the mediation of recording has the effect of imbuing authority on the recorded performance in a number of ways:

> First, the performance acquires significance as a message targeted not at a mere individual, but at millions of anonymous potential listeners. Second, the absence of the musicians during the playback of recordings sets them apart socially.... Third, the availability of the recorded performance in commodity form testifies that someone with some degree of control over the technological media of sound reproduction...has already evaluated the performance and deemed it worthy of recording and distribution. Fourth, the performance carries a price tag....[12]

The selection of any recording for release involves a series of value judgments on the part of those involved in the production process as to why this performance in particular should be released. In Jarrett's case, as we will see later, other performances from the same tour were recorded, so the decision to release this particular one is also a decision to reject others in favor of this one. The effect of singling out the Cologne performance is significant, because as Butterfield suggests, it imbues the performance with authority, implying that this one is more important than others given around the same time.

Recently, theorists working in the relatively new field of performance studies have debated what "liveness" might mean. As Philip Auslander suggests, live performance is usually seen in binary opposition to recorded performance; one is authentic and unmediated, the other artificial and highly mediated.[13] But as Butterfield suggests, the distinctions are nothing like as clear as that. A theoretical view outlined by Peggy Phelan is that once a performance is "saved" it is no longer a performance, but something else altogether.[14] What is important, Auslander suggests, is how notions of live and mediatized come to be understood in particular historical and cultural contexts. Even if we have to treat a live recording as a mediatized artwork, what are the cultural values attached to the idea of liveness in a jazz recording? Put differently, how does the idea of liveness affect the discourse surrounding such a record?

This is one of the points from which my examination of *The Köln Concert* begins. Rather than think of it as a live record, I will consider how the reception and subsequent understanding of the recording has come to imbue it with qualities of liveness. This stems from the manner in which Jarrett was performing, stressing his reliance on an improvisatory aesthetic whereby each performance was a unique, ephemeral event. In this way, the recording encourages the listener to experience the record as a live performance, and to ignore the processes of mediatization involved. The recording in this sense works as artifice, camouflaging its own nature as contingent on a set of technological and cultural processes, instead acting as the medium for a particularly expressive and personal performance, produced in a singular nonrepeatable context.

This might seem to subscribe to the mythologization of live recording. But I want to try and acknowledge the highly personal way in which many listeners have engaged with this recording. At the same time, I will seek to contextualize the performance, to emphasize how it needs to be understood within a social, historical, and cultural context. This implies a number of approaches that work outward from the recording as object. This is not to suggest working *away* from the recording, but rather setting up a dialogue between text and context, in order to attempt to break down the rather artificial barriers these notions imply. But how might this work for *The Köln Concert*?

Jarrett was one of any number of American musicians working in Europe in 1975, whether performing as a touring artist or living there. There were good reasons for American artists to visit Europe at this time because of the audience they could attract, and indeed for Jarrett because of the German ECM label for which he was recording. As I explore in Chapter One, *The Köln Concert* is, in part, a document of the engagement between an American artist and a European audience. It serves as a microcosm of a much larger transatlantic dialogue, among musicians, audiences, critics, recording companies, journalists, and so on.

The questions I address in Chapter Two regard the record's critical reception, and its sales during the first few years following release. Jazz historians tend to view the 1970s as a decade when the music was pushed to the fringes of popular culture, the only exception being forms of jazz fusion, regarded by parts of the jazz press as a blatant turn to commercialism. I argue that the reality is far more complex than this, and that those musicians who were willing to take on board the values and fashions that had become important to a young generation found that their music was appreciated by the same audience. Jarrett's creativity was understood by part of his audience in terms of an aesthetic of liberation. This was an enormously important cultural concept of the time, and *The Köln Concert* came to be seen as an articulation of this aesthetic.

In Chapter Three I develop an understanding of how Jarrett forged a particular kind of approach to solo piano playing. The Cologne performance was part of an ongoing project in Jarrett's career that involved playing solo piano concerts. His first solo piano recording, the 1971 *Facing You*, was but one of a number of solo records made by pianists for the ECM label. Among the others are records by Chick Corea and Paul Bley, with rather lesser known albums by Steve Kuhn and Richie Beirach. In Chapter Three I show how these solo recordings demonstrated an emerging conception of form in jazz. This was a post-songform conception, but at the same time it avoided the open-ended form often used in "new thing" jazz, and the highly structured compositions played by many of the fusion bands. This was a kind of form that was malleable, and yet structured, allowing freedom for the musician to extend aspects of the piece, while creating a sense of proportion and structure for the listener. This understanding of form would be enormously important for Jarrett's solo concerts.

Chapter Four begins an analytical approach to the music of *The Köln Concert*. In doing so I start by surveying a number of theoretical perspectives on free improvisation and Jarrett's music. I suggest that crucial to understanding Jarrett's music is the idea that the act of listening is to participate in a sense of shared time with the improviser, and thus I focus attention on understanding the expressive function of some of the kinds of music Jarrett plays in his solo improvisations. Chapters Five and Six deal with the two main improvisations on the Cologne record, along with the encore, listed as "Part IIc" on the record. These chapters contain some detailed musical discussions, but along the way they develop ideas about how the music functions expressively, how it employs some formal archetypes that are familiar within jazz and some that are not. Also crucial is the idea that the music can be said to be expressive, on the basis of an understanding that it affords a certain kind of listening experience.

In Chapter Seven I move beyond the immediate reception of the record to consider its longer-term legacy. In doing so, I confront the idea of the record's relationship to New Age music. I consider what this might mean, and I look at how there is another kind of reception history to the record, a reception that points to how recorded music offers a range of potentials to listeners.

CHAPTER 1

LIVE RECORDINGS PREMISE their appeal on the idea of the listener
being able to eavesdrop on a time and place, to become a participant in
a performance in a way that is, by definition, impossible. Quite naturally,
then, the visual presentation of such recordings usually plays heavily on
the details of when and where. Keith Jarrett's *The Köln Concert* is no different from most other live recordings in this respect. Not only does the
album title itself name the place, but the track names ("Köln, January 24,
1975, Part I," etc.) conflate place and time. Most of Jarrett's solo concert
releases follow the same pattern; the album title names the place (*Paris
Concert, Carnegie Hall Concert*, and so on), and frequently the track title
includes the date. For the Cologne record, the photographs on the front
and back covers of the record show Jarrett at the piano. Visible behind
him on the back cover is a building, indicating the photograph must
have been taken at an outdoor performance, rather than at the Cologne
Opera House. As it happens this is the only solo concert release that

includes a photograph of Jarrett performing on the front cover, that is until *The Carnegie Hall Concert* of 2006. This mode of presentation can be seen to articulate a philosophy of production that avoids artifice or narrative while presenting only the bare factual information. These production aesthetics have become intrinsically associated with the ECM label, but at the same time as they appear to boast their transparency, they disguise as much as they reveal.

For one thing, the emphasis on the place and time of performance almost inevitably obscures the process of production. We learn nothing about other performances from the same time, which may or may not have been recorded. The recording might seem to document a performance and a context, but it also distances other performances, by singling out that moment in time. Accounts of the Cologne concert, such as those I have already mentioned, rarely make any mention of the other performances Jarrett undertook on his European tour in January and February 1975. It is almost as if Jarrett had traveled to Europe solely to play at the Cologne Opera House. Such is the price we pay for the documentary function of recording; the act of documentation can serve to distort our view of the context with which we are presented. This serves as one facet of a critique of the role of recordings in the writing of jazz history that has emerged in recent years.[1] But recordings are not necessarily hampered by such limitations. In order to place and discuss a recording we need to begin by moving away from it, to circle around and back again. In this case, resisting the lure of the recording's doorway to time and place means looking to a sense of a larger musical, cultural and transnational context, which can help to contextualize what it is the recording is capable of doing. In this chapter, then, I want to consider how Europe came to be so important for Jarrett's career, in particular in the development of his solo playing, and the manner in which that mode of performance came to be formulated during the early part of his career as part of regular trips across the Atlantic.

JAZZ IN EUROPE

Europe has generally had a minor role to play in standard narratives of jazz history. Like the bit-part actor, it appears suddenly in certain scenes and quickly vanishes into the background. This is hardly surprising of course. Jazz is inextricably associated with America, not only as its spiritual and cultural home but, according to many commentators, as the one place that provided the diasporic conditions under which it could flourish. As E. Taylor Atkins points out in one of the relatively few books seeking to challenge such assumptions, "practically all jazz discourse rests on the premise of American exceptionalism."[2] By the 1960s, Europe was well established as a potential destination for American musicians who were looking for performance opportunities outside their native country. There was by this time a network of jazz clubs in major cities, an increasing number of jazz festivals, and the emergence of European record labels, arguably the major factors needed to support a community of expatriate professional jazz musicians. Given the distance spanning the two continents, most musicians would never have considered crossing the Atlantic for a single engagement; it made sense as a destination only if one were going on tour. But by the 1960s, it was clear that Europe held other attractions, as a place not only to perform but also to live.

During the decade that followed, a significant number of musicians made the trip across the Atlantic to take up residence on a new continent. In most cases, this turned out not to be a permanent move, but the length of many stays was considerable. Famous examples include saxophonists Johnny Griffin, Steve Lacy, and Ben Webster; arranger, theorist, and composer George Russell; and the Art Ensemble of Chicago.[3] Other musicians ended up looking for work while in Europe, and taking what opportunities came along. Pianist Paul Bley describes in his autobiography a long tour of Europe in 1966, built on a series of gigs, each resulting from the other, and recording five albums in as many months for European labels.[4]

Of course, it is all too easy to assign cause and effect to explain the increasing appeal Europe seems to have held for musicians. One might cite the narrowing market for jazz in America during the latter part of the 1960s, which had an impact especially on musicians who were playing what parts of the jazz press called "new thing" music. And then there was the fact that many musicians cited the improved conditions they found in Europe. Pianist Cecil Taylor, known as very much part of the American avant-garde, spoke in a debate convened by *Down Beat* magazine in 1966 saying, "I worked in conditions that I can't work in here. Every major city I went to in Europe, I had a radio show, a television show, and lectures, as well as working in clubs. And they even paid me for the lectures."[5] The reality of the attraction Europe held is best understood as a confluence of factors, namely the emergence of a viable network of clubs, radio stations, jazz festivals, and record labels, as well as an enthusiastic audience in Europe, which allowed musicians to work there.

The ironies involved in this movement of musicians across the Atlantic were not lost on the American jazz press. *Down Beat* had long contained short reports from European countries, sometimes listing significant events, reporting the main performers at certain festivals, and often relaying news of how American performers working abroad were being received. Musicians such as Dexter Gordon and Bud Powell, relatively well known to American audiences, naturally prompted such an approach to reportage. But in the early 1970s it is possible to detect the theme of Europe emerging again and again. Not only was there some comment in the jazz press on the success musicians enjoyed on leaving America, but readers also had the chance to hear about this directly via the medium of interviews with musicians. In the June 22, 1972, edition of *Down Beat*, which carried an interview with Gordon, the saxophonist spoke about the difference between the American audience and the Europe one, and the fact that Europe felt like a relaxed place to live.[6] The trip to Paris undertaken by the Association for the Advancement of Creative Musicians was also well reported in the American jazz press, as Ronald Radano points out.[7]

It is instructive to compare this situation to the German jazz press. No German jazz fan or critic could have been unaware of the idea that it was the American musicians who represented the strongest, most direct link to the roots of jazz—the "real thing," in other words. It is possible to imagine that for them American jazz was the most authentic expression of the music. And yet the German jazz press of the 1970s gives nothing of that impression. The German jazz fan had, by this time, a considerable choice of musicians to see in performance, including visiting American groups and individuals, American musicians living in Europe, and a range of German bands. In the month of January 1975, when Jarrett was touring Germany and Switzerland, among the groups touring Germany were Chick Corea's Return to Forever, Larry Coryell's group Eleventh House, pianist Champion Jack Dupree (a resident in Europe by this time), German musician Albert Mangelsdorff, and a package of British "trad" groups including Monty Sunshine's Jazzband and Max Collie's Rhythm Aces. The amount of jazz being broadcast on German radio stations was considerable, ranging from traditional jazz to recordings from the Berlin Jazz Festival. This meant that the German jazz fan could regularly hear recordings of American musicians performing live. Although the German publication *Jazz Podium* occasionally ran news items or features that were in themselves reports from American festivals, or news of *Down Beat's* readers' or critics' polls, at the same time there was enough coverage of European musicians and events there to make it quite clear that the German scene was, by that time, well established and even flourishing. In essence then, the picture that emerges is of a well-informed German jazz scene, populated by enthusiasts who were able to keep up to date with the activities of leading American musicians by way of a magazine such as *Jazz Podium*, as well as through radio broadcasts and live performances. But at the same time, they were able to hear European musicians performing, and indeed the pages of *Jazz Podium* indicate very clearly that European musicians were seen not as imitators of Americans but as forging a distinct sound in their own right, which deserved to be treated on its own merits, regardless of comparison to its transatlantic forebear. This can be seen as part of a broader movement, described by Mike Heffley as representing European jazz moving from an approach that can be broadly characterized as imitative of American jazz to something distinct and original.[8]

JARRETT IN EUROPE

As a young player, Keith Jarrett would have quickly adapted to the idea of Europe as a viable region for touring and generating publicity that could be useful in America. Jarrett's first major gig was with the Charles Lloyd group. Lloyd was a saxophonist who formed his own band in 1966 and took on the help of experienced producer and manager George Avakian. The story of how Avakian promoted this band to enormous success, taking them to Europe in order to create enough momentum to have any effect on the American scene, has been recounted by Ian Carr and Stuart Nicholson.[9] From the very beginnings of his time in the Lloyd band, Jarrett was touring Europe. In 1966 the group played engagements in Sweden, Denmark, Norway, and France. A year later, when Jarrett had formed his own trio with drummer Paul Motian and bassist Charlie Haden, the liner notes to his first record, *Life Between the Exit Signs*, by Avakian (who was also Jarrett's manager by this point) proudly proclaimed that "One could fill this back cover with extraordinary press comments about Keith Jarrett, culled from 18 countries within an 18 month time span (he has made six European tours in 1966–67 as a member of the Charles Lloyd Quartet)."[10] The manner in which Avakian cites Jarrett's acclaim as international provides a strong indication as to the way he saw the situation: this international touring served as a means to help establish Jarrett's reputation in America. Avakian's approach was, in retrospect, particularly enlightened for the time, recognizing the opportunities that international touring created for the jazz musician. But at the same time, the implication still seemed to be that what was important was the American audience. The point of all this touring for Lloyd (and presumably the same strategy applied to Jarrett's trio) was to establish a reputation in America that would allow Lloyd sufficient performance and recording opportunities to sustain a career as a band-leader and musician in his own right. Europe seemed to be a means to an end, rather than as an end in itself.

It is clear that by the early 1970s Jarrett was an artist working interna-tionally. He was by no means unusual in seeing Europe as affording him career opportunities that could be pursued alongside his work in Amer-ica. In a piece on Jarrett from *Down Beat*, January 20, 1972, Joe Klee wrote of how Jarrett had been working frequently with his trio, "mostly in Europe, where the gigs are."[11] This is a useful point with which to begin, as it helps to establish why and how Europe and ECM provided the means by which Jarrett could pursue solo playing—a project that, arguably, would not have been so easy if undertaken solely within the American market.

JARRETT AS SOLO PIANIST

The development of Jarrett's career as a solo pianist, and as an artist whose reputation came to be built in large part on his solo concert performances, was mainly as a result of the transatlantic nature of his career during this time. A key part of this was the relationship Jarrett began with German record producer Manfred Eicher and his new ECM label. After Eicher founded ECM, he began asking a variety of musi-cians to record. Sometimes these were spur-of-the moment actions, after he had heard a particular performance. Jarrett's relationship with ECM seems to have begun with a letter, which according to Ian Carr Jarrett received in 1971. This was at a time when Columbia records had terminated Jarrett's recording contract. Eicher apparently explained who he was and proposed a number of recording projects to Jarrett, with the pianist selecting the solo project. Jarrett has recounted that one of the possibilities Eicher suggested was a recording with fellow pianist Chick Corea and two bassists.[12] Jarrett's first recording for ECM was made possible because he was on a European tour with Miles Davis, and thus he was able to record a solo piano album in Oslo called *Facing You* that marked out an enormously important moment in his career.[13] But Jarrett was not the only pianist Eicher was asking to record solo. As I will explain in Chapter Three, Jarrett's recording was part of a kind of unofficial set Eicher assembled, along with work by Chick Corea and by Paul Bley.

The roster of musicians who recorded for the label in its early days demonstrates a transatlantic view of jazz. The American musicians who recorded for the label were not in many cases "names" in their home country, and neither were the Europeans, at least until later on. Eicher seems to have been looking for a certain kind of approach and attitude from the musicians he recorded, as well as being keen on fostering collaborations between European and American musicians.

Jarrett's position as an ECM recording artist was to prove enormously important in Europe, where ECM had better distribution than in America, at least until the mid-1970s. The exposure that he had gained in Europe by touring with Charles Lloyd and Miles Davis meant he was well known to a wide audience. ECM's activities were not simply down to producing and distributing records, but included organizing concert performances in Europe for some of their artists. Eicher did this first for Jarrett in 1972, as part of an arrangement with Jarrett's American manager Avakian, under which Jarrett was contracted to the American Impulse! label but also allowed to undertake special projects for ECM.[14] The fact that Jarrett was recording simultaneously for two labels was not lost on American critics. Some expressed the view that the Impulse releases during this time were formulaic compared to the ECM outputs.[15] Jarrett explained in a 1975 interview with *Melody Maker* that "the music that's recorded for Impulse (and/or Atlantic) is consciously presented with the environment of America, where it is most widely distributed. And the music that I record with ECM isn't—I don't mean this in a slightly more universal, very large sense, but it's that Europe is not as isolated as America."[16] These remarks imply that Jarrett was certainly aware of a difference in approach in his work for these labels. The inference that the American scene was rather insular might be seen as a signal that Jarrett set himself particular restrictions when recording for Impulse. And yet the irony is that for some contemporary musicians the music Jarrett made with his American quartet has been more influential than his output on ECM.

As part of the first concert tour Eicher organized for Jarrett in 1972, he undertook a number of solo performances, the most notable being one he recounts thus: "I actually had a spot at a festival in Heidelberg, it was a jazz festival....I just had a lot of songs at my disposal, my own and other people's. And when I went to start to play, somehow the songs attached themselves, in other words there were like transitional periods, and then I'd be playing another song. That evolved, I think very slowly, into the transitions taking over and the songs disappearing."[17] Though there is only Jarrett's word to go on that this constituted the first solo concert, it is worth attempting to verify some facts. Establishing a date for this performance is somewhat difficult, but there are other factors that help to pin it down. In an interview with *Down Beat* in December 2008, Jarrett recalled playing the Heidelberg set after Austrian pianist Friedrich Gulda.[18] Gulda was, at this time, playing with the group Anima, who certainly performed at the 1972 Heidelberg Jazztage, and excerpts of the group's performance appeared on the MPS records release *Heidelberger Jazztage '72*.[19] That places Jarrett's performance some time between June 2 and June 4, 1972. Further confirmation comes from an unlikely source. In a travel article in the *Oakland Tribune* from August 1972, the author describes taking a trip to Heidelberg and noting that a jazz festival was running there, mentioning Jarrett's name specifically.[20] Nor was Jarrett the only American musician playing solo at this festival. The following year Paul Bley appeared, and played a long solo piano improvisation, mentioned in *Jazz Podium*.[21]

Jarrett was already in Europe at this point with Charlie Haden and Paul Motian and seems to have played at the Alba Regia Jazz Festival in Hungary on June 3. As to why some solo performances should have been scheduled in the midst of a sequence of dates Jarrett was playing with his trio is not exactly clear. It is possible to infer Eicher's influence here, given his importance in organizing dates for Jarrett, and perhaps an ambition to translate the music of *Facing You* to the concert stage, even if only in terms of format. That Heidelberg was not a one-off is confirmed by the fact that Jarrett seems to have played other solo performances in Europe later that summer. These included at least two concerts in Sweden and one at the Molde Jazz Festival in Norway. There also seems to have been a solo performance in New York at some point in late 1972, which, according to Avakian (Jarrett's manager at the time), was held at the Mercer Arts Center.[22] This concert was reviewed by Illhan Mimaroglu in *Down Beat* in January 1973. Mimaroglu wrote that "when it all ended he addressed the audience to say that this was an experimental concert, and that the response (which had been wildly enthusiastic) was as good as it had been elsewhere in the world."[23] Bob Palmer noted in a record review for *Rolling Stone* in December 1972 that Jarrett was "gravitating more and more toward solo playing," citing a recent unaccompanied recital, possibly the same concert to which Mimaroglu referred.[24] Avakian's own account of the development of the solo concert format is somewhat different from Jarrett's. He recounts how Jarrett came to him with the idea, and he put together the concert, at which incidentally Jarrett met Manfred Eicher. However, given that the New York performance seems to have been in late 1972, and Jarrett had played a number of solo performances in Europe earlier that year, including Heidelberg, Avakian's account does not quite tally.

But what of Jarrett's account of stumbling across a way of structuring solo sets at the Heidelberg performance by segueing from one number to another? The surviving bootleg recordings from the Stockholm and Molde concerts just a little later that summer do not give this impression on first hearing. However, one Jarrett expert, Simon Savary, has spotted two pieces buried within the Molde concert. The first, half an hour into the first part of the concert, is the composition "The Magician in You" from the album *Expectations*, which Jarrett had recorded the previous October in New York. The other tune seems to be a version of "Rainbow," which Jarrett would record some years later, in 1976, on the album *Byablue* but which seems to have made occasional appearances in his set lists around this time. The Stockholm performance also contains an embedded piece that would reappear as the encore to the 1973 Bremen concert (from the *Solo Concerts* recording) and later as the encore to the 1984 Tokyo concert recorded on the video *Last Solo*. Though this may not entirely support the account Jarrett gives of the Heidelberg performance, it does at least constitute evidence that at this time the solo concert improvisations incorporated existing compositions. As we will see later on, this is not something peculiar to the very early solo performances, and it raises a whole set of issues about how these concerts have come to depend on expectations associated with improvisation. The music of the Stockholm and Molde performances is episodic to a degree, but in that respect they are much like most of Jarrett's solo performances. It may have been that Jarrett developed his approach to this new format with considerable verve, and this part of the process has simply not been documented on recordings.

There is interesting evidence from rather earlier suggesting that the genesis of the solo concert idea, and specifically the idea of segueing via transitional material between composed pieces, might have been something Jarrett had been working with for a time. A tape exists of a Jarrett solo set performed in Paris in 1970, around the same time he was on tour there with Haden and Motian. It is rather hard to place the context from the recording. The atmosphere sounds like that of a club, and the scattered and sometimes muted applause along with background conversation indicates a context far from the formality of the later solo concerts. The range of the material Jarrett performs is striking to say the least, comprising what might be described as a rather chaotic mishmash of styles. Jarrett performs on Fender Rhodes electric piano, guitar, flute, and acoustic piano, as well as singing in a couple of places. In addition to performing some of his own pieces, and longer selections that seem to have been completely improvised, there is also a version of George

Harrison's "Here Comes the Sun" and part of the Beatles' "Lucy in the Sky with Diamonds."[25] The overall intent seems perhaps closer to the music of projects such as *Restoration Ruin* (Jarrett's so-called folk rock album of 1968) and *Ruta and Daitya* (recorded with Jack DeJohnette in 1971). The concert certainly pre-dates the 1972 performances Jarrett is talking about, because there is no attempt to integrate the different pieces, and the enormous diversity in style and instrumentation makes it hard to imagine them as a combined whole. This rather eclectic musical approach has been largely forgotten in Jarrett's output, partly because it was replaced by the appearance of greater musical coherence during the early part of the 1970s. Yet it is worth remembering, because it says much about the kind of conception of music Jarrett and many other jazz musicians of a younger generation had—a theme I will return to in Chapter Two.

If the 1972 solo dates in Europe seem to have been shoehorned in with some trio engagements, Jarrett's solo performances in Europe in 1973 were quite different. It was the solo concert tour of 1973 that produced the first formally documented performances, with the release of the *Solo Concerts* recording, which had an enormous critical impact on the jazz world. Jarrett performed in a number of venues across West Germany, Switzerland, Finland, and Italy. The two concerts in Bremen and Lausanne, documented on the *Solo Concerts* LP, were recorded respectively in March and July 1973. But he was not in Europe throughout this period, as Ian Carr tends to imply.[26] Instead it appears Jarrett returned to America for a number of engagements in June of that year, including the Newport Festival and a booking for his quartet (with Paul Motian, Charlie Haden, and Dewey Redman) at the Village Vanguard, before returning to Europe for more solo dates in July. That logistical fact highlights the kind of juggling act typical of Jarrett's schedule during this period, keeping both his quartet and solo work going, and on both sides of the Atlantic.

THE 1975 SOLO CONCERTS

In addressing the January 24, 1975, performance in Cologne, it is worth examining a little more of Jarrett's performing itinerary at the time. Table 1.1 offers a list of Jarrett's known engagements from the end of 1974 through March 1975.[27] The European tour formed the major part of Jarrett's work at this time. The ECM brochure for the 1975 European tour makes an interesting statement in this regard. It features a series of quotes from various publications about Jarrett, including *Down Beat*

(U.S.), *Melody Maker, New Musical Express* and *Let It Rock* (UK), *Die Weltwoche* and *Badener Tagblatt* (Switzerland), and *Sounds* (Germany). On later pages, there are lists of accolades (*Down Beat* Record of the Year for 1974, and the *Swing Journal of Japan's* Grand Prix du Disque for the same year). The inclusion of these citations from a number of publications is perhaps revealing of how Jarrett was being presented as an international recording artist.

When he returned to the United States in February after the European tour, he had further solo concert engagements, but they do not appear to have been part of a tour in the way that the European performances were. Before leaving for Europe he had fulfilled a residency at New York's Village Vanguard Club with his quartet. But visiting Europe to perform and record was, by now, an established part of his way of working. In the summer of 1974 he played a solo tour, taking in dates in France and Italy, including the Umbria Jazz Festival at Perugia, where a solo performance was filmed. A year later he would be touring Europe with his quartet, while also taking part in a number of recording sessions in New York.

ECM's role in organizing concerts and tours for its artists, even in the relatively early days, is often forgotten. In this case, the story behind the first concert in Jarrett's tour is worth recounting. Jazz enthusiast Hans-Dieter Klinger visited ECM's office in Munich around 1972 (at the time situated behind the Elektro-Egger record store owned by Karl Egger, a businessman who had helped fund the ECM label in its early days) and enquired about booking Jarrett.[28] ECM had told Klinger that they received many expressions of interest about performances by ECM artists and could forward details to him. So it was that he received information about the forthcoming 1975 solo tour Jarrett was undertaking and managed to secure a venue in Kronach, a town in Bavaria with a population of between ten and twelve thousand people. Jarrett's performance there was sold out, and Klinger recounts that they could have filled the hall twice over, such was the demand. This in itself is testament to Jarrett's reputation in Germany at this time. Jarrett had been on a skiing holiday in the Alps prior to this performance and apparently arrived feeling ready to go, having had a break from performing. On arriving, he asked to see the piano straight away and expressed his approval (to Klinger's huge relief) but indicated that the piano tuner might have to return to work a little more.

The Cologne performance was the fifth date on Jarrett's European tour, and the middle of a three-night run where he was playing in Lausanne, followed by Cologne, and then Baden in Switzerland. The Cologne concert was attended by a number of the city's music critics, invited by

TABLE 1.1   Jarrett engagements, 1974/5

Date	Venue	Format
October 16, 1974	Lisner Auditorium, George Washington University, Washington, DC	Solo
October 19, 1974	Bucks Play House, New Hope, PA	Solo
October 23, 1974	Newport Jazz Festival	Solo
October 31, 1974	Sanders Theatre, Harvard University, Cambridge, MA	Solo
November 26– December 1, 1974	Village Vanguard, New York	Quartet
December 14, 1974	Koussevitzky Arts Center, Berkshire Community College, Pittsfield, MA	Solo
December 22, 1974	Tyrone Guthrie Theater, Minneapolis	Quartet
January 17, 1975	Kronach, Germany	Solo
January 20, 1975	Villingen, Germany	Solo
January 21, 1975	Freiburg, Germany	Solo
January 23, 1975	Lausanne, Switzerland	Solo
January 24, 1975	Cologne, Germany	Solo
January 25, 1975	Baden, Switzerland	Solo
January 29, 1975	Graz, Austria	Solo
January 31, 1975	Hamburg	Solo
February 2, 1975	Bremen, Germany	Solo
February 3, 1975	Munich	Solo
February 5, 1975	Paris	Solo
February 13, 1975	Poughkeepsie, NY	Solo
February 20, 1975	Evergreen College, Olympia, WA	Solo
March 13, 1975	Royce Hall, UCLA, Los Angeles	Solo

March 16, 1975	Lincoln Center, NY	Guest soloist in "3/4," a Carla Bley piece conducted by Dennis Russell Davies
March 21, 1975	Toronto, Canada	Solo
April 20, 1975	Given Auditorium, Colby College, Waterville, ME	Solo

Brandes.[29] It certainly seemed to have an impact on those who were there at the time, not just later on when the record was released. On the journey from Cologne to Baden, made again by car, Jarrett and Eicher (who were traveling along with Jarrett's wife Margot, and their son Gabriel) listened to playback of a cassette of the Cologne performance.

The Baden performance, held in a school auditorium as part of a regular series of concerts, was again sold out, according to journalist Bruno Rub.[30] Although Swiss Radio recorded a number of the concerts in this series, for some reason the Jarrett performance was not recorded. Just a week later, his performance at Bremen in Germany was taped, and subsequently broadcast on German radio. Rub quotes one local critic writing about the Baden concert indicating that Jarrett threatened to cancel if there was so much as one click of a camera during the performance. This kind of attitude is one that has been associated with Jarrett in much more recent times. Critical reactions from the local reviewers were rather divided, one questioning whether Jarrett was a prophet or a pianist, and others finding the musical results somewhat mixed.

Following the Baden performance, Jarrett and his party took a little break, staying at a hotel there, according to Rub. It was here that he met the Swiss journalist Peter Ruedi, and they conducted an interview for a feature on Jarrett published in the German *Weltwoche* journal. Ruedi mentioned in his piece on Jarrett that the pianist seemed tired.[31] Indeed, according to Rub, Jarrett wrote in the guestbook to the hotel of looking for an apartment in the area for later in 1975, indicating perhaps an intention to return for a vacation. Whatever the truth, on Jarrett's return to the United States he gave a number of interviews in which he indicated that he wanted to scale back his performing activities to concentrate on composition.[32]

Jarrett's performance in Hamburg was well covered by the *Hamburger Abendblatt* newspaper. A preview of the concert that ran in the paper on

January 30 cited Jarrett as the most-talked-about pianist of the time, and it outlined the influence of his previous solo records.[33] The Hamburg performance received a fulsome review from the paper, noting that at the end members of the audience stared, as if mesmerized by Jarrett.[34] The examples of Kronach, Baden, Cologne, and Hamburg then indicated that Jarrett's fan base in West Germany and Switzerland was strong. Not only was it the case that specialist jazz publications were willing to laud him as an important figure, but his solo performances on occasion took prominent place in mainstream media, such as the *Hamburger Abendblatt*. And to the German press, the Cologne performance, recorded by ECM, would have had quite a different significance than for an American audience. Cologne was after all local, part of the national circuit. And perhaps for that reason critics promoting an upcoming Jarrett appearance would speak of the fame of the legendary Cologne performance rather than necessarily the recording, in essence conflating the two.

The single performance in Paris that Jarrett undertook as part of this 1975 tour seems perhaps rather detached from those performances in Germany, Switzerland, and Austria, but it is not without precedent. Jarrett would have had some experience of playing in Paris, as he would of many of the other venues on his tour.[35] The 1975 concert was held at the Théâtre de Champs-Elysées, incidentally the same night that German pianist Joachim Kühn was performing solo at Studio 105 in the city. The reviewer for *Le Monde* mentioned a Jarrett performance at the 1974 Antibes festival, fearing "lengths and breaks and affectation."[36] Most likely the reference here is to a Jarrett solo performance at the Antibes festival the previous summer, where he was one of the five pianists the festival had scheduled to play at the event. Leonard Feather made reference to this performance in a piece for the Los Angeles Times in August 1974, saying that "Jarrett's recital, just 50 minutes long, was played without interruption. His was the least overt display of technique among the five pianists, yet his astonishing resources and improvisatory control placed a limitless variety of imagery at his disposal."[37] Perhaps it was the length of the Antibes performance that had put off the *Monde* reviewer, although he also gave the impression of familiarity with some of Jarrett's solo work.

These European performances also stand in sharp contrast to the solo concerts in America, which I have listed as part of this itinerary (Table 1.1). The major difference here is that the European performances were part of a tour organized by Eicher, who was dealing only with Jarrett's European performances. His American activities were being organized by his manager, Brian Carr. The result is that the American solo concerts were not organized as tours but took place often rather sporadically. This may have reflected something of the scaling back on Jarrett's part that he had talked about in March 1975 to *New York Times* critic John S. Wilson. His remarks to Wilson indicated his attitude regarding where he should play solo concerts: "My instinct tells me not to do a solo concert in New York now.... I don't know why. But I've followed my instincts for several years, and I just know it would be wrong."[38] In addition, Jarrett said of Europe that "musicians classified as jazz performers are more apt to be accepted on the same level as classical musicians than in the United States."[39] These remarks bring us back to the fact that Jarrett was an American musician who had become used to performing in Europe almost as much as he did in America. Clearly the solo concerts had developed in Europe, more so than in America. So it was that Jarrett found himself with, as it were, one foot on either side of the Atlantic Ocean, keen to capitalize on his status in Europe as a concert artist and his relationship with ECM records, but also continuing a musical relationship with American musicians on the club scene in the United States, while performing solo concerts at a variety of venues there. And as I will explore in the next chapter, the enormous commercial success of the Cologne recording was a function of the American audience, because the recording came to appeal to that audience in a very specific way.

CHAPTER 2

AS I ARGUED at the very start of this book, understanding how *The Köln Concert* came to be measured as a commercial success requires moving beyond simply reeling off sales figures, tempting though that may be. One facet of this approach is to attempt to understand and account for the particular kind of following that the record built. To do so requires considering some questions about the demographic of the jazz audience in America during the 1970s, specifically about the audience buying Jarrett's records.

The sales that *The Köln Concert* enjoyed during the 1970s were, in part, a result of Jarrett's strong following in America. Although the record was born out of a trans-Atlantic dialogue as I have suggested, the demographic of the audience who bought the record in America is significant for what it says more generally about jazz during the 1970s. Although this chapter will focus particularly on the record's reception in America, this is by no means to denigrate the importance of how it was received elsewhere in the world, not least in Europe where it was created. I will argue that the factors contributing to its enormous success were most clearly found in America, the country in which Jarrett lived and worked, and with which he was most associated.

The Cologne record not only had wide appeal but came to be something of a cultural symbol. There was an important resonance between the values Jarrett articulated regarding his music making, reinforced in a number of ways by the presentation of the album, and wider ideas about creativity and the self that permeated parts of American culture at this time. The record's appeal was in part due to its ability to articulate values that were highly appealing, especially to a younger audience. But to begin, I want to consider how the jazz audience of the 1970s has usually been understood in relation to a highly polarized, stylistic distinction.

STYLE AND CROSSOVER IN 1970S JAZZ

There has long been a widely articulated sense that jazz in the 1960s was being pushed to the margins by the increasing popularity of rock, with consequences that musicians and audiences would have to deal with during the following decade. As Eric Porter says, "Musicians, critics, and fans affiliated with jazz had their share of uncertainty during the 1970s.... Declining record sales, club closures, and racial tensions were among the many issues that caused hand wringing about the state of the art form and its future."[1] These economic and cultural conditions are often cited as part of the reason for the advent of a kind of music that took influences from both jazz and rock, usually labeled as "fusion." As Stuart Nicholson puts it, "in the social context of the time, jazz-rock was not only inevitable, it was necessary for the music's survival."[2] But where Nicholson sees fusion as a necessity born out of the hard realities of economics, historians have sometimes seen it in a rather different light. One view has sidelined music that falls under the banner of fusion as a blatant play to commercialism, compromising musical and artistic standards for profit.[3] Considering Jarrett in terms of these fault lines serves to highlight how much more complex the cultural situation was at the time than these accounts suggest. The framing of this debate through the binaries of jazz and rock, and "selling out" as representing a shift from one camp to the other, imposes a clear-cut distinction that is extremely difficult to sustain. It is worth beginning by thinking about this from the perspective of a young generation of jazz musicians who were starting their professional careers at the cusp of the 1960s and 1970s, of whom Jarrett was one. For such musicians, the music they identified with during the 1960s was as likely to be by the Beatles and Bob Dylan as it was Miles Davis or John Coltrane. Stuart Nicholson quotes Larry Coryell to this effect: "We were saying, We love Wes [Montgomery], but we also love Bob Dylan. We love Coltrane, but we also love the Rolling Stones."[4] In Jarrett's case, his identification with Dylan's music was made explicit through a critically panned album from 1968 called *Restoration Ruin*, on which he played guitar and sang. As I have already mentioned, a bootleg recording from a 1970 Paris performance has Jarrett playing guitar and singing in the midst of a solo piano set. Jarrett had also recorded a version of Dylan's "My Back Pages" on his 1968 trio album *Somewhere Before*, while a bootleg recording from Denmark in 1969 has a live version of the same tune along with Dylan's "Lay Lady Lay."

That this generation of musicians should have identified with the popular music of their time is unremarkable. But it is necessary to note this, simply because the 1970s have become contested territory for some historians. The idea that jazz musicians could allow an awareness of popular musics to permeate their approach can be found writ large throughout jazz history. During the late 1960s and 1970s, this manifested itself as more than just a musical nod to rock. Rather than don the traditional lounge suit, dinner jacket, or tuxedo of the jazz musician, the likes of Gary Burton and Coryell grew their hair long and wore contemporary, informal clothes, as Stuart Nicholson recounts.[5] In a piece in *Rolling Stone* on the 1968 Monterey Jazz Festival, critic John Burks contrasted Burton's "motorcycle jacket, jeans and flowing straw-color hair" to what he described as the overall weariness of the festival, questioning whether jazz was ready "for the Rest home."[6] This tapped into a sense, sometimes articulated by critics of the time, that mainstream jazz was a music of a bygone age, standing only for nostalgia. If Coryell and Burton were adopting this stance in the late 1960s, one can find a similar approach, as David Ake points out, with the cover art to the Pat Metheny Group album *American Garage* (1978). The artwork sees the band pictured in jeans and t-shirts, rehearsing in a garage—hardly a typical image for a jazz group.[7]

Jarrett's experiences in the 1960s playing with the Charles Lloyd group at venues such as the Fillmore Auditorium in San Francisco attest to much the same attitude as that exemplified by Coryell and Burton. The group's introduction of the Beatles' "Here, There, and Everywhere" in their live set, as documented on *Love-In* (1966), indicates a view of jazz very different from the idea of a stylistically autonomous music that some histories seem to presume. To a young generation of musicians, it was not that jazz and rock represented two sides of a stylistic fault line all musicians had to navigate, but that it seemed perfectly natural to play a kind of music acknowledging both styles, without setting out to create some sort of hybrid. There was considerable cultural capital to be gained by jazz musicians who could demonstrate a musical approach free of dogma and respect for stereotypical classifications. As we will see, Jarrett benefited enormously from what could have been described as "crossover" appeal.

The idea of fusion as it was used in the music press during the 1970s seems to have been a highly mobile marker, certainly not the kind of rigidly fixed category that historians have subsequently employed. Musicians who could be labeled as playing fusion were often identified by their use of electric instruments. In the case of Jarrett's contemporaries, Herbie Hancock and Chick Corea both fitted fairly neatly into this category (although this is to overlook the challenging acoustic jazz Corea recorded with his band Circle). Jarrett had played electric organ and electric piano while with Miles Davis, although he has said repeatedly that he hated playing those instruments. Around the same time, he also played electric piano on the *Keith Jarrett & Gary Burton* album from 1970, as well as on the little-known *Ruta and Daita* (1971) with Jack DeJohnette. But by 1973 Jarrett was publicly railing against the use of electronic instruments, describing himself as being on an "anti-electric-music crusade."[8] These views were widely quoted in a variety of contemporary press features on Jarrett. Even so, for a musician apparently skeptical of the electric instruments that characterized the work of the biggest-grossing fusion acts of the time, such as Chick Corea's Return to Forever and the Mahavishnu Orchestra, it was significant that Jarrett won the *Rolling Stone* jazzman of the year award in 1973.[9]

It might be easy to presume that as a publication whose natural inclination in stylistic terms was toward rock, *Rolling Stone* would have tended to favor one of the jazz musicians associated with taking jazz in that direction, but not so. This accolade seems to have been particularly important, and it gave Jarrett credibility to a certain audience in a way that praise by *Down Beat* would not have. Take, for instance, a mention of Jarrett that year in the *Harvard Crimson* student newspaper. Writer Peter M. Shane noted, "A few months back, I goofed by underplaying a local concert by electric pianist Keith Jarrett. Rolling Stone named him jazz man of the year, and his concerts and albums are winning unanimous raves. Live and learn."[10] The labeling of Jarrett as an electric pianist may simply have been a mistake based on the fact that Jarrett had previously played electric piano with Davis. But it also reveals what seems to have been a widespread lack of agreement on whether Jarrett should be considered a fusion musician or not. Some publications were happy to list him alongside contemporaries such as Hancock, Corea, and John McLaughlin, all well known for their use of electric instruments. On the other hand, Jarrett was sometimes mentioned alongside McCoy Tyner, a pianist known for working entirely in the acoustic realm, and by and large avoiding the standard stylistic routes that fusion implied. So even though Jarrett's views on electric instruments were sometimes used as a means of differentiating him from a number of his contemporaries, equally he was compared with them for other reasons. Jarrett was far from being the only jazz musician interested in deliberately forgoing electronics. Some such as McLaughlin would return to acoustic instruments after a lengthy involvement with electric instruments. Guitarist Ralph Towner and his group Oregon came to be known as potent symbols of acoustic jazz, Towner's reputation being particularly strong in Germany, where he played a number of solo performances around the same time as Jarrett.

One of the themes that emerge from press coverage of Jarrett regards his status as a jazz musician. A certain amount of this is, as we will see, down to his efforts to distance himself from the label of jazz. In the commentary to the 1975 *Village Voice* Critics' Poll, Robert Christgau noted that "Keith Jarrett is the favorite jazz musician of rock critics, but didn't amass enough votes because several felt he didn't qualify for a pop poll."[11] In this instance Jarrett is the only jazz musician mentioned in a piece that discusses the likes of Joni Mitchell, Stevie Wonder, Bob Dylan and James Taylor. In the trade magazine *Billboard's* listings on Jarrett albums, a similar kind of theme emerges. Reviewing the 1976 *Arbour Zena* record, which featured Jarrett with Jan Garbarek, Charlie Haden, and string orchestra, the commentary said, "Dealers: Jarrett's playing can be reminiscent of a [sic] ersatz classical setting, lending opportunities to sell him to neoclassical and/or classical buffs."[12] More explicitly, on the album *Staircase*, the publication wrote: "The pace of this offering is slow compared to what usually clicks, but Jarrett's jazz is so classical it works....Dealers: Appeal to rock, jazz and classical listeners."[13] *Billboard's* notices on other Jarrett albums emphasized his reputation both as a consistent seller of jazz records and as someone with a crossover appeal to record buyers. These critical maneuvers served to establish Jarrett's connections with jazz but also positioned him as eclectic. This was a position Jarrett benefited from, as James Lincoln Collier suggested in an article in the *New York Times* in 1979: "A good many jazz critics and fans deny that what Jarrett plays is jazz at all....This eclecticism is no doubt responsible for perhaps the most interesting aspect of Jarrett's career, which is that his followers are not solely jazz buffs, but are drawn from the whole spectrum of music—classical, pop, rock and folk."[14]

That these stylistic labels caused problems when applied to Jarrett is an important point to make. Naturally, such labels serve a highly practical function, one more important for the music press and industry than for musicians. But there was a potential cachet available for musicians who could be seen to be associated with jazz, without the implications of a tradition-bound, insular approach. It was not that jazz was unpopular with a younger audience, as is sometimes presumed, but that musicians had to demonstrate a conception unfettered by narrow stylistic conceptions of jazz.

The Köln Concert benefited enormously from Jarrett's placement in these terms. It is worth considering the record's review in *Rolling Stone* in the first instance. *Rolling Stone* began their review like this: "Keith Jarrett is…the most commercially successful of the younger crop of ex-Miles Davis pianists. He hasn't penetrated the pop Top Ten like Herbie Hancock but his recordings of solo acoustic piano improvisations…have sold better than the efforts of most players who'd hoped that plugging in would help them 'relate.'"[15] Of course, *Rolling Stone* was a publication whose readership would have been far less likely to consider themselves jazz aficionados, explaining why mainstream chart success should have been such an item worthy of note.[16] The *Rolling Stone* review distinguishes Jarrett from players associated with electric instruments, and by extension from fusion. But at the same time he benefits from this distinction, because the inference is that he does not engage in the shallow gestures of musical fashion. At the same time the review identifies Jarrett as an artist enjoying commercial success, not a jazz musician struggling to find an audience. The reason for this is made clear: "He never sounds avant-garde or alien but he always sounds fresh—and he seems to be well on his way toward transcending category entirely and becoming a popular performer in the truest and broadest sense."[17]

The mention of Jarrett's eclecticism in positive terms is significant. This is a theme that is woven richly through accounts of his playing at this time and is found in a number of critical reactions to *The Köln Concert*. For example, in a roundup of the year's best records in the *Montreal Gazette* at the end of 1975, critic Juan Rodriguez listed *The Köln Concert* among his favorites of the year, noting beforehand, "regrets to the realms of country music, folk and mainstream and experimental jazz."[18] These are styles he had excluded from his list, the implication being that the Jarrett record was neither mainstream nor traditional jazz and could be placed in a list with records by Bob Dylan among others.

Writing for *Down Beat*, Neil Tesser saw the record as a "pinnacle" for Jarrett in terms of solo work. He identified two unlikely sources of musical inspiration: voicings drawn from Russian romantic composers such as Rimsky-Korsakov, as well as folk music. On the latter, Tesser commented that "the piece abounds in English and Scottish-sounding folk melodies, bagpipe drone voicings in the left hand, ringing church chimes and organ-pipes in the right."[19] As we will see in Chapter Five, the musical language of the first part that Tesser discusses here has musical implications that do indeed go far beyond jazz. But Tesser also invokes a trope of emotionalism here, writing that "Jarrett is an out-of-the-closet romantic, but moments of sentimentality are rare: his transportive beauty glides on starkly touching incisions to the psyche's emotional lifeline. His solo art remains a unique entity in music, and *The Köln Concert* is its most moving, most telling exposition." Writing in *Melody Maker*, Steve Lake took a similar kind of stance: "The delicacy of his touch, as on the fourth side of this set, is almost tear jerking, leading one to suspect that beneath all the bravura Jarrett is just another hopeless romantic."[20] Lake did contrast the record to *El Juicio* by Jarrett's American quartet, the other record he was considering in the review, summing up the difference in tone by saying, "By contrast, it's strictly hands clasped and kaftans on for *The Köln Concert*." The reference in this case seems very much of its time, while also pointing to the rarefied atmosphere of the solo concerts as we will see later. When John S. Wilson reviewed the record for the *New York Times*, he noted Jarrett's two recording careers, in Europe and America. His rather humorous metaphor to describe Jarrett's piano style, as like "Chopin and Art Tatum steaming together downstream in a canoe," summed up a kind of stylistic mix highly unusual for jazz.[21] This eclecticism was presented as a positive aspect, part of Jarrett's crossover potential.

The question of these highly romantic traits in Jarrett's music is a significant one. In 1976 German critic Joachim-Ernst Berendt published an article entitled "Jazz and the New Fascism" in *Jazz Podium*.[22] Berendt's piece was prompted in part by an article by Susan Sontag on Leni Riefenstahl, a film maker and actress known for being a Nazi propagandist. Berendt's anxiety about the emergence of what he saw as a new kind of fascism in jazz and rock has to be viewed against the enormous sensitivity there was in Germany to the possibility of the arts being appropriated for such ends.[23] His consideration of the aesthetic of beauty is interesting, given how far away this kind of discourse is from that in the American press of the time. He identifies Jarrett along with Corea, McLaughlin, Tyner, and Weather Report as examples of a kind of new romanticism. For Berendt it was not just the appropriation of the aesthetic of the beautiful, and the uncomfortable resonances it had with the kind of art Riefenstahl was credited with, that was a concern, but the fact that for him this was also a neutering of jazz, stripping away the political and social engagement it had demonstrated during the previous decade. Even though Berendt's argument is rather hard to pin down, it is nonetheless a fascinating piece. Coming at a time when Jarrett's solo releases held very high status in Germany, and indeed only some months after the release of *The Köln Concert*, it is difficult not to speculate that Berendt had Jarrett's solo piano work very much in mind when mentioning him.[24]

The role Jarrett's solo work played in this debate further emphasizes the complexity of the transatlantic dialogue I have described. It is tempting to consider the reception of *The Köln Concert* against two differing aesthetic backgrounds, one European, one American. Jarrett's own admission that the music he made for the Impulse label was conceived differently from what he recorded for ECM might seem to give weight to this interpretation. But the reality is that Berendt's views proved controversial, and they were certainly not indicative of a wider suspicion of Jarrett's solo work. Indeed, the subsequent popularity of *The Köln Concert* in Germany suggested that the aesthetic Berendt was suspicious of was perhaps one that was highly appealing.

These debates aside, by the end of 1975 *Time Magazine* were listing the record as one of the best of the year's jazz releases, alongside the Art Tatum solo recordings.[25] Because of the record's release that autumn, it did not feature in some publication's lists until the following year, including *Billboard*, where it was listed as the third-best-selling jazz album of the year, behind releases by Grover Washington Jr. and George Benson.[26] Citing reviews and critical commentary is but one part of the picture though. What of the audience who would come to listen to and purchase Jarrett's records, especially *The Köln Concert*?

JARRETT'S AUDIENCE

Michael Segell, writing in *Rolling Stone* in 1978, provided a neat stereotype of the contemporary jazz fan at the end of the decade: "To the surprise of no-one, the demographics of today's jazz consumer reveal an older, more mature fan: mostly male, college-educated, and between twenty and thirty."[27] He quoted an executive from Columbia Records who identified this generation as one that would have grown up with rock and then broadened their musical tastes into their twenties and thirties. In the following year, Mikal Gilmore would write in the same

publication of jazz reaching its "broadest audience in over a generation."[28] But the question of how this generation came to be listening to
jazz is an interesting one. Was it the case that those forms of jazz termed
"fusion" had the effect of introducing a younger generation to jazz? It is
tempting to think so, given the widespread sense in the press that by the
end of the 1970s jazz was making something of a comeback in the United
States. But a look at the evidence suggests that throughout the 1970s
there was a young audience ready and willing to engage with jazz, and
not necessarily just those forms of jazz that played to rock aesthetics.

By the start of the 1970s, Columbia Records had identified the possibility for marketing jazz to a young, white, rock-oriented audience. This
was the strategy they famously took with Miles Davis.[29] For Columbia
this meant advertising Davis's music using contemporary lingo to make
the music seem hip and relevant, along with harnessing the potential of
the underground press. But the irony here was that Davis himself wanted
to play to a black audience and was deeply suspicious of the move to
market his music this way. Columbia's strategy doubtless had some success, but it points to a much larger issue. Even far beyond the marketing
strategies of a major label such as Columbia, there was ample evidence
that a young white audience was willing to engage with jazz, though it
could be easily put off by such marketing. One of the keys to understanding this audience is what Segell alludes to: they would most likely have
been college educated.

A piece by critic Will Layman, published online in 2008, begins with the
arresting statement, "The Koln Concert alone lifted more 1970s college
dorm parties into the ether than all of the marijuana east of the Mississippi."[30] Layman may make an interesting if anecdotal assertion, but it is
one that indicates something about the audience for this record at the time.
As far back as his stint with Charles Lloyd, Jarrett would have been used to
playing on college campuses. Lloyd's group made a point of cultivating a
young audience, performing at the Fillmore Auditorium in San Francisco
before Miles Davis went the same direction, garnering a following on college campuses where Lloyd liked to play the role of the guru/mystic.[31]
Critical writing on the group emphasized their potential to attract and
engage with what jazz critics were wont to term disparagingly a "hippie"
audience. Thus Bill Quinn's review of the 1967 album *Forest Flower* (recorded live at the 1966 Monterey Jazz Festival) noted the audience's approval, commenting, "How many times do the hippies get off their behinds
for a jazz performance?"[32] Clearly the experience of the Lloyd group was
that it was possible to engage with a young audience by performing at
venues such as the Fillmore and at universities and colleges.

Until the 1970s, jazz might have seemed an unlikely candidate for inclusion in college and university courses. But in that decade the situation began to change markedly. In a pair of 1971 articles in the *Music Educator's Journal*, Paul Tanner surveyed the provision of jazz as part of college courses, concluding that it was increasingly seen as a subject worth inclusion in music courses.[33] Of the institutions Tanner surveyed, more than 80 percent had their own jazz bands. In a 1982 article, Bryce Luty outlined the growth in jazz education seen during the sixties and seventies, through college students being allowed to take a jazz ensemble as part of their study.[34] The evidence may not have pointed to a solid place for jazz on curricula, and indeed David Ake has recently asserted that it was not until well into the 1970s that jazz became widely available for study.[35] But even if it was not formally part of the curriculum, there is much evidence of an upsurge of interest in jazz among a student audience. This much is plain from commentary on jazz in record and concert reviews and other reportage in student newspapers of the time. Student-organized concerts flourished, and many major jazz names performed at campuses. Some, like the Stan Kenton band, made it something of a mission to tour schools and colleges promoting an interest in jazz among youngsters.

The assumption might be that a college-age jazz audience would have consumed the jazz fusion being produced by musicians and groups such as Herbie Hancock, Miles Davis, and the Mahavishnu Orchestra. This was the music major labels such as Columbia were marketing to them, seeking a crossover audience who would identify with jazz. And there is certainly evidence that for this audience such acts were major draws, garnering reviews and mentions in student publications and airplay on student radio. But alongside these acts, other names held prominence, particularly those of Jarrett and McCoy Tyner. Jarrett might have still enjoyed the kudos of being a Davis sideman, but the fact that he was best known during this time for his work with acoustic groups (both the American and the European ensembles) and as a solo pianist left no doubt that this was a musician not interested in the lure of electronics in the same way as keyboardists such as Hancock and Weather Report's Joe Zawinul.

Around the midseventies, it is quite clear that among Jarrett's American engagements a significant number took place at educational institutions, as part of student-run festivals or concert series. By mid-decade at least, he was regularly performing on campuses in America as part of his engagements. By way of a brief sample, his itinerary for the years 1974 and 1975 took in performances at, among others, UCLA, Princeton, and Harvard (see Table 2.1).

TABLE 2.1   Jarrett engagements at Colleges and Universities, 1974–5

Date	Venue
October 16, 1974	Lisner Auditorium, George Washington University, Washington, DC
October 31, 1974	Sanders Theatre, Harvard University, Cambridge, MA
February 13, 1975	Vassar College, Poughkeepsie, NY
February 20, 1975	Evergreen State College, Olympia, WA
March 13, 1975	Royce Hall, UCLA, Los Angeles
March 21, 1975	Convocation Hall, University of Toronto
April 20, 1975	Colby College, Waterville, ME
October 4, 1975	Iowa Memorial Union (sponsored by the University of Iowa)
October 15, 1975	McCarter Theater, Princeton University, NJ

A look at how Jarrett was described in the student press indicates what it was about his music that appealed. A review of *The Köln Concert* in the *Daily Collegian* (Penn State University) on February 2, 1976, noted that "There is an accessibility to Jarrett's solo efforts that is gaining him wide popular support as well as critical acclaim. This music is not avant-garde, it is above all melodic, and this makes the 'Koln Concerts' [sic] an excellent album for new jazz listeners as well as older fans."[36] The explanation that Jarrett's music was not avant-garde seems to have related to a wariness about free jazz on the part of some writers on the college scene. What is interesting is the reference to "melodic," code perhaps for the idea that this was accessible music, "new jazz listeners" presumably being a way of referencing some of the student readers of the publication. Beyond the fact of Jarrett's performance activity at college campuses, combined with evidence that his music was being reviewed in college newspapers, more widely it is possible to find evidence that the demographic for his records and concerts was notable for its percentage of younger members, at least compared to a typical jazz audience of the time. In a review of the 1976 Newport Festival by Amy Lee from the *Christian Science Monitor*, there is a description of Jarrett's performance with Jan Garbarek and Charlie Haden, partly of music they had recorded on the *Arbour Zena* LP (1976). Jarrett had taken to the stage after Benny

Goodman's performance, and Lee's comments made light of the markedly different demographic: "It was packed later for the Keith Jarrett concert, this time with a nearly 98 per cent young audience."[37]

Other evidence from the period indicates musicians and critics noticing the same general trends emerging. In a piece on the 1973 Monterey Jazz Festival, *Rolling Stone* noted how young listeners seemed to be drawn to a range of jazz not confined to the fusion of groups such as Mahavishnu or Return to Forever, but including acts such as Jarrett, Sun Ra, Davis, Pharoah Sanders, and Tyner.[38] It was certainly the case that concerts by fusion groups drew legions of young fans.[39] But it was not only this kind of music that was drawing such fans. Dave Brubeck, for instance, noted in 1975 how the audience coming to see his group (which included his sons) was "80 or 90% high-school and college age."[40]

By the mid- to late seventies, jazz was far from being in decline, instead expanding its audience. A number of press notices pointed this out, citing statistics that along with the growth of jazz within education testify to something of a turning of the tide. In a 1975 article, "Jazz on the Comeback Trail," Ira Gitler wrote about students on a jazz history course he was teaching, commenting on their openness to different forms of jazz.[41] He also remarked on a revival in ragtime and earlier forms of jazz, and the huge commercial success Hancock had enjoyed with his *Headhunters* record. Other stories of the time charted a surge in jazz record sales, and the record circulation of *Down Beat*.[42] One evident aspect of this upsurge in jazz was that it was not restricted to fusion but included acoustic jazz. Jarrett was well placed to be associated with this kind of trend, not least because of his pronouncements on electric instruments, and his advocacy of the acoustic piano. Leonard Feather, writing in the *Los Angeles Times* in 1977, questioned whether Jarrett would become the standard bearer for a new kind of jazz: "Are we about to enter a brave new world of acoustic music to which young, rock-reared audiences can relate? If we are to judge by the financial and artistic success of Jarrett's venture, he will be the man to lead us through the gates."[43]

On the release of *The Köln Concert* in the autumn of 1975, it was set to appeal to a young audience who were following Jarrett, many of whom might have already come across his music through the *Solo Concerts* LP, notices for which appeared in any one of a variety of press publications including *Rolling Stone* and *Down Beat*. The fact that the *Solo Concerts* record had already sold well in America indicated that the proposition of releasing improvised piano music was not as foolhardy as it might have initially seemed. The popularity of the Cologne recording derived in part from how Jarrett was able to appeal to this young audience, by virtue of being seen as a contemporary jazz artist who was not indulging in the obvious strategy of "plugging in." But this is only one small part of the story of what happened in the years following the record's release. One of the central points of this book is that a large part of the importance of *The Köln Concert* recording stems from how it came to be seen as articulating a set of values that had enormous cultural resonance at the time.

THE IMPROVISING BODY

Reactions to Jarrett's performances during the 1970s almost invariably made mention of the spectacle of his physicality while playing, something the listener familiar only with his records might not have appreciated. Portrayals of his performances in the press often took the form of detailed verbal descriptions that paint a vivid picture. Take for instance John S. Wilson writing in the *New York Times* in March 1975: "Keith Jarrett plays the piano as though he were dancing with it. He is seated when he starts, but his first few notes lift him from the piano stool, his body buckling as he threatens to disappear under the keyboard only to pull himself up to his full height, descend briefly to the stool and rise again, leaning into the piano in a half crouch."[44] This kind of account, paralleled by countless others in reportage throughout the decade and even beyond, attempts to give the reader a description of the physical contortions Jarrett seemed to put his body through when performing. Linked to such verbal accounts were photographs, often used for publicity purposes. Some of the advertisements for Jarrett solo concert performances in the American press used a photograph of him performing. He is sitting upright, leaning back, his arms stretched straight out to the keys and his head pressed downwards into his chest, so that he looks much further from the piano than standard representations of pianists would allow.

Nor was it the case that these representations were confined to press items on Jarrett. During the 1970s two programs featuring his playing aired across America. One was a broadcast of a 1977 outdoor solo concert recorded in Shelburne, Vermont. The film showed Jarrett performing on a grand piano, in the twilight of a summer evening, with an audience sitting cross-legged on the grass listening carefully. A second was a documentary entitled "At the Top," which aired extensively during 1976. Importantly, both programs would have given viewers access to the sight of Jarrett performing.

Associated with these descriptions of Jarrett's physicality were press accounts that linked these kinds of bodily motions to mysticism. Herbert Aronoff wrote in the *Montreal Gazette* in October 1974, "Jarrett's approach seems not so much based in jazz as it does in the mystical chanting of the yogis. The young pianist works with his instrument... rising from the bench, twisting and contorting his face and his body, rocking and weaving as though in a trance."[45] In the same newspaper in 1979, Juan Rodriguez wrote, "By turns, he'll do 'The Twist' at his seat, swivel his head like a spinning top, stand up and hunch over the piano, or crawl under it.... He has thrown himself totally to the winds of spontaneous creation. To him, it's a religious mystic experience and, if that seems as though he's thumbing his nose at the world, so be it."[46] Not all accounts read Jarrett's movements this way, though. One reading was that Jarrett's movements were akin to a sex act, and his vocalizing was reminiscent of orgasm. In the press at least, it is the mystical reading that seems to have been more commonplace.[47]

More and more is being recognized about the importance of visual imagery in how we understand, and listen to, musical performance. Although we might consider the issue of visual imagery specifically with regard to live performance, there are good reasons to think also about recorded music, where the listener's attention is drawn toward a sound object that is, by nature, disembodied. Sound recordings are often described in terms of the loss of physical presence caused by the mediation of technology. This fact is often used to deem recorded music as second best to the experience of live performance. But jazz scholar Tony Whyton argues that it is possible for jazz recordings to "lead us to a position where the potentially negative reactions to physical loss are reversed. Both despite and because of the lack of physical and visual presence, new forms of mystique can be created... through the power and influence of jazz icons."[48] Similarly, Philip Auslander argues with regard to rock recordings that "our ability to visualize the performance of rock music as we listen to it is dependent on the availability of visual artifacts that show us what the musicians look like in performance."[49] Visual representations of Jarrett are particularly important because they have the potential to point to a set of preconceptions against which listeners heard this music.

These images of Jarrett playing were potent, not simply because they added a visual dimension to perceptions of his artistry but because they became conflated with a crucial aspect of how he was seen, and that was as an improviser. Even before Jarrett began playing solo concerts, he had been articulating his ideas about music and aesthetics quite forthrightly, whether through interviews, liner notes to records, or lectures to audiences. This ideology has sometimes been seen as no more than egotistical posturing, and indeed by the end of the 1970s some critics were openly questioning Jarrett's views.[50] In the liner notes to the *Solo Concerts* release, Jarrett included a self-authored liner essay, apparently as a way of explaining the music. It resorted to existential philosophizing, in this manner: "I don't believe that I can create, but that I can be a channel for the Creative. I *do* believe in the Creator, and so in reality this is His album through me to you, with as little in between as possible on this media-conscious earth."[51]

Around the same time that *Solo Concerts* was released, in a 1974 interview with Bob Palmer in *Down Beat*, Jarrett spoke in a similar way, although in rather more straightforward language: "Now I'm at the point of knowing it's there, I'm not in a position to describe where it comes from. I've been letting it happen all by itself so much that I'm looking at it as something completely independent of me, which it really is. I'm just transmitting it."[52] This and the liner notes outline an attitude to improvisation based on both spontaneous creation and the idea of a creative source external to the performer. From portrayals of Jarrett in the press, the overall impression that emerges is one attesting to a highly romanticized conception of the artist as genius. That is, the spectacle of Jarrett's body in performance was related to the creative endeavor he was undertaking. The physical contortions came to be signs of the creative project, of struggle with the process, or with his "muse," as Bob Palmer put it in 1972.[53] This is in many respects very close to the modern origins of the classical recital in the nineteenth century, as tied up with the idea of genius, the performer presenting himself or herself before an audience to be appreciated for the display of extraordinary abilities.

As a result of these preconceptions about Jarrett's music making, coupled with his own statements on creativity and improvisation, the solo concert performances came to be highly ritualized. Ritual can be thought of as a highly repetitive series of actions, in which no two performances are the same. Christopher Small's adoption of the term in his book *Musicking* draws on anthropological theory to understand ritual as the enacting of a set of relationships and concepts through the language of gesture.[54] As Small suggests, in this sense public performances are just as ritualized as religious ceremonies.

At the same time, given the liner notes to the *Solo Concerts* recording and Jarrett's own pronouncements on his creative endeavors, the solo piano records he made are not simply documents of performances but artistic manifestos, articulations in music of the aesthetics he was expounding. This has to be seen as part of a movement that finds its origin during the 1960s, at the point when musicians involved particularly in avant-garde or "new thing" jazz became conscious of the importance of justifying and even theorizing their music. The manner in which this discourse took place was often abstract, couched in terms emphasizing the spiritual, manifest most famously in John Coltrane's poem on the liner notes to *A Love Supreme*, which, as Lewis Porter demonstrates, Coltrane "plays" in the final part of the suite.[55] This turn to the spiritual is part of what Ronald Radano views as a reclaiming of the links between African-American music and spirituality.[56] The increasing reliance musicians placed on the written word as a means of articulating their philosophy was also linked to what Eric Porter sees as an "investigation into the power and function of improvisation."[57] But even though Porter identifies a series of African-American musicians who used the written word to articulate such philosophies (Yusef Lateef and Marion Brown among others), it would be a mistake to confine this trend to black musicians. We can, for instance, find Chick Corea in the pages of *Down Beat* in 1971 outlining a philosophy that reflected his growing interest in the ideas of L. Ron Hubbard, which would lead to Corea's involvement in Scientology.[58]

Placed within this tradition, *The Köln Concert* emerges as part of a conscious artistic project Jarrett was undertaking, which had its roots in these ideas about jazz performance, improvisation, and creativity. It also drew on the conceptions of his music making in visual terms that were circulating widely. But to understand how this record found a following, it is also necessary to confront the wider context of the 1970s, and to understand a little more about an audience that was crucial in forming the success of the Cologne recording over the years that followed its release.

MUSIC AND IDEOLOGY IN THE 1970S

Historians writing about American culture in the 1970s often relegate the decade to the status of that which came after the 1960s. Given the political and social upheavals the 1960s witnessed, from the dramas that played out over the civil rights movement to the emergence of a counterculture that found visible expression at an event such as the 1969 Woodstock festival, the 1970s seemed overshadowed by everything that had gone before. The decade has sometimes been viewed as representing the demise of an idealism that found all kinds of voices in the 1960s, from the rhetoric of the Port Huron statement, penned by a group of student radicals, to Martin Luther King's speech in Washington, D.C., in 1963. This idealism went hand-in-hand with what is often described as a far-reaching disaffection among the youth population, disaffection manifest through protests against the Vietnam War and rejection of what historians often term the "affluent" postwar society. The result was a yearning for alternatives, as expressed through lifestyle, clothing, culture, and belief systems.

One particularly important theme of the 1960s was the burgeoning interest in new expressions of religion, mysticism, and thought. This interest took a variety of forms, incorporating not only an upsurge in traditional Christianity but interest in Eastern religions, Zen philosophy, and the occult. Some commentators have seen this as part of the need to forge a new kind of identity, articulating an alternative to the norm. But all these themes can be interpreted as directed toward a particular kind of philosophical and personal goal, tied up with the aims of what is sometimes given the umbrella term "the movement." Contemporary commentators were apt to describe it in that way, as two accounts published in 1970 demonstrate. Charles Reich's *The Greening of America* and Theodore Roszak's *The Making of a Counterculture* both attempt to look for common themes behind the counterculture of the time.[59] For Reich this begins with the notion that the individual is stripped of individuality and right to self-expression through what he calls the "technocratic society." Reich describes a number of stages of consciousness being developed through the counterculture, of which Consciousness III was a new attitude toward living in which the self was of defining importance. Roszak examined what he saw as a demand for "a deeper examination of that dark side of the human personality which has for so long been written off by our dominant culture as 'mystical.'"[60] His remit took in such areas as the growth of Zen Buddhism and humanist psychology as found in the work of the therapist Paul Goodman. Roszak suggested that all of these themes were directed toward a sea change in understanding what constituted consciousness, and how this might affect the individual.

A number of commentators on the 1970s see these themes developing in the new decade. Peter Clecak's book-length study *America's Quest for the Ideal Self* takes as its central premise the idea of an underlying search that extends from the sixties through the seventies.[61] This search, as Clecak sees it, took a variety of forms but had at its heart the idea of personal fulfillment, however that was expressed. It was grounded in the wish for an alternative that a generation growing up in the 1960s articulated, but it found a whole host of manifestations. Other commentators on the decade see much the same story, even if articulated in more localized ways. Bruce Schulman points out how one of the best-selling books of the decade, *Jonathan Livingston Seagull*, by Richard Bach, dramatized a similar theme, that of the individual being able to surpass, or even transcend, the banality of everyday life, seeking a truer and more fulfilling alternative.[62] Another articulation of this idea was in the grittier realism of escape envisaged in some of Bruce Springsteen's work of the seventies, notably *Born to Run* (1975).[63] Springsteen's music was all about the dream of escape from the banality of an everyday working life, rather than a utopian impulse. This escape was one of the themes Tom Wolfe identified in his famous satirical essay "The Me Decade and the Third Great Awakening."[64]

Is it too much of a leap to suggest that *The Köln Concert* articulated this idea in some way, or at least acted as a symbol of the impulse to escape aspects of the technocratic society for an alternative? Perhaps it is. But the emphasis on the physical spectacle of Jarrett performances, the rhetoric used in describing them, and Jarrett's eschewing of electric instruments makes clear that a specific kind of interpretation was common currency. The imagery of Jarrett performing, coupled with this ideology, made his performances richly symbolic, affording a range of interpretations that extended far beyond the music. All of the many representations of Jarrett available to listeners in the 1970s, from press reports to television broadcasts, attested to the same idea. The visuals of the televised Vermont performance presented a musician performing without any of the trappings of technology in the great outdoors, and directly to his audience. This spoke of a form of music that was pure and unadulterated by technology. Combined with the potent ritualized context that put the idea of improvisation center stage, as a kind of music making that could be spontaneous even to the point of catharsis, all these factors made Jarrett's solo performances resonant cultural symbols.

Even the album art on Jarrett's records seemed to suggest the same thing: simple and understated, with little in the way of imagery. But the images that are provided with the Cologne recording are telling. There is the front cover, picturing Jarrett at the piano, with his head bowed into his chest and his eyes closed.[65] The image in itself is richly evocative. The bowing of the head is an attitude typically associated with prayer and religious devotion. And yet film footage shows that Jarrett could also be a highly exuberant and physically expressive performer. This sparse visual style supports a musical aesthetic characterized by avoidance of the paraphernalia of technology, or at least that associated with much music at the time: amplifiers, synthesizers, effects pedals, and so on. Acoustic music came to function as an important symbol during the seventies of a kind of literal and metaphorical unplugging, a liberation from the confines of technocratic society, to use Roszak's term.

If we can understand the cover art of *The Köln Concert* in terms of an ideology that emphasized lack of mediation, and the importance of spontaneity and the self, what has the music to do with this? One of the key areas of interest for musicologists considering rock music from the late 1960s and 1970s is the idea of psychedelia, and the associations music had with altered states of consciousness, specifically those induced by hallucinogenic substances. Musicologists such as Sheila Whiteley have explored some explicit connections between music and psychedelia. For Whiteley, much music of this time can be understood as analogous to altered states; that is, the music serves as a kind of sonic representation of "tripping out."[66] Very often in her argument this comes down to electronic manipulation of timbre; the "spaced out" effects one hears in psychedelic rock serve to represent a chemically induced state. But does this imply that it is only rock that can be read in this way, or that a countercultural articulation of a higher state can be revealed only through the kinds of devices Whiteley identifies?

In her study of the music of Led Zeppelin, Susan Fast suggests that music has the potential to create profound meaning through the act of listening, rather than meaning being encoded in the music.[67] For Fast, equating acoustic phenomena with drug use is too narrow and confining. What is of significance instead is how music can enact ideas about transcendence, liberation, and spiritual experience for its listeners. Is it possible to understand *The Köln Concert* against this background, and does the music offer any potential for such experiences? This is a question I will return to later on, after a detailed account of the music of the recording. This is not the end of the story, however. As we will see much later on, *The Köln Concert* came to be associated with the 1970s and its culture to such a degree that it, and some of Jarrett's music, came to be seen under the category of 'New Age', a move that Jarrett has tried to resist.

CHAPTER 3

OVER THE SPACE of a year, between 1971 and 1972, three American pianists recorded solo albums in an Oslo studio for the relatively new ECM record label. Paul Bley, Chick Corea, and Keith Jarrett were the pianists, and the resulting albums, Bley's *Open, to Love*, Corea's *Piano Improvisations Vol. 1* and *Piano Improvisations Vol. 2*, and Jarrett's *Facing You* are now regarded as signaling a revival of interest in solo piano within jazz. Solo concerts would come to be Jarrett's calling card, something that seemed to bring him more attention than any other facet of his musical endeavors, not least through the success of the Cologne recording. But it is worth examining how the musical conception we find documented on *Facing You* relates to the form Jarrett's solo concert improvisations took when they first appeared on record with the *Solo Concerts* release in 1973. To do that also involves considering the Corea and Bley albums because, taken together, they make an important statement not only about the viability of solo piano as a format but about how a solo musician could engage with the idea of form.

The note to Bill Dobbins's published transcription of Corea's first *Piano Improvisations* album begins, "Along with solo recordings by Keith Jarrett and Paul Bley, they [the Corea recordings] inspired a renewed interest in the art of solo piano improvising, which had been largely neglected since the era of Earl Hines, Fats Waller, Teddy Wilson and Art Tatum."[1] The view Dobbins expresses is one that has been widely articulated elsewhere, namely that these recordings represented something of a renaissance for the idea of solo piano in jazz, following a period of comparative neglect.

Jazz has usually been thought of as a group activity, born of the interaction between musicians in the moment of performance. The manner in which musicians interact while performing not only is an important stylistic component of jazz but can come to be part of a larger narrative of musical progress. Perhaps for this reason solo playing has been relegated to a footnote in jazz history, subservient to a narrative in which ensembles dominate. This is reinforced by the association of playing solo with contexts such as restaurants, or intermissions between nightclub acts. Performance in such contexts often suffers from its association with the idea of background music, designed to be purely functional and not to be given (or to solicit) attention. But to invest in this stereotype is to forget that solo piano performance has been present right from the inception of jazz, particularly through the tales of the "ragging" pianists such as Jelly Roll Morton, and those who held court in Harlem during the 1920s such as Willie "The Lion" Smith.

There is of course a considerable gap between 1920s Harlem and the Oslo studio in which Bley, Jarrett, and Corea recorded during the early 1970s. And there is a danger of presuming that in the intervening years there was little in the way of solo piano music being recorded, as perhaps Dobbins and others imply. But this is not necessarily the case. Although the vast majority of recorded jazz in the intervening years was dominated by groups and big bands, there were still a significant number of influential solo piano records made. Any list of these records would probably include Dave Brubeck's *Brubeck Plays Brubeck* (1956), Jackie Byard's *Blues for Smoke* (1960), Lennie Tristano's "Descent into the Maelstrom" (1953) and *The New Tristano* (1962), Bill Evans's *Conversations with Myself* (1963), and Thelonious Monk's *Thelonious Himself* (1957).[2] Many of these players could have been considered modern or progressive when they produced these records; this much is certainly true of Brubeck, Byard, Evans, and Tristano. The Brubeck album is particularly interesting because, aside from a couple of versions of fairly well-known Brubeck tunes ("In Your Own Sweet Way" and "The Duke"), it comprises pieces that do not conform to the usual approach one might expect a pianist to take in this context. Brubeck described in the liner notes how the pieces were "primarily sketches—a skeletal framework upon which to improvise, to express a mood or emotion or stimulate musical ideas."[3] Interestingly, his liner notes also outline in some detail an artistic ethos behind the record. Brubeck describes three levels of creativity in jazz, the highest of which involves an effortless and spontaneous performance, while the lower ones involve the recycling of formulae and use of a "backlog repertoire." Jarrett has confirmed in an interview with pianist Ethan Iverson that he heard the *Brubeck Plays Brubeck* recording when he was a teenager, and other than that recording and some Lennie Tristano "there wasn't much else for modern playing in a solo context."[4]

The association both the Brubeck and a number of the Tristano records have with a kind of experimentalism is interesting. Tristano's 1953 recording "Descent into the Maelstrom" was an early exercise in overdubbing, predating Evans's *Conversations with Myself* album, which is regarded as a classic of the genre.[5] For Tristano, who engineered the session himself, the process of recording was a means by which he could document a distinctive musical approach. *The New Tristano* from nearly a decade later eschews song structures and reflects Tristano's distinctive formulaic experimentation. Barry Ulanov's liner notes explain to the listener the kinds of exercises Tristano practiced, pointing out where the results can be heard on some of the tracks.[6] Even if the solo piano format as a medium for recording was not widely used, it does seem to have functioned to allow musicians leeway to experiment in how they constructed pieces. Making solo piano records was not to document on record the kinds of playing pianists might have done if playing solo sets; instead it prompted musicians to conceive of the recording as a chance to evolve their own approaches to solo playing, free from the confines of song forms. There may not be evidence Jarrett was deliberately trying to emulate any of the musicians I have mentioned in his approach to the solo record, but his awareness of their work demonstrates the degree to which he was at least aware of the precedents.

PLAYING SOLO

The idea of making solo records has become particularly associated with ECM as a result of these early 1970s recordings. But it is all too easy to overplay the label's influence in this respect. It is possible to argue that the slew of recordings that seem to emerge from other pianists in the wake of the Jarrett/Corea/Bley efforts might have formed an artistic response that would establish the significance of the ECM releases in setting a precedent for solo piano as a recording format. But before Manfred Eicher organized any solo sessions for ECM, there was already wider interest in solo playing in jazz emerging from some quarters as a response to the implications of the avant-garde movement in jazz of the 1960s.

Andrew Raffo Dewar has pointed out a number of important factors to consider in this reemergence of solo playing during the late 1960s and early 1970s.[7] There is, first of all, the legacy of certain streams of jazz that had moved beyond song forms to what is sometimes called "open form." Dewar uses the term "post-songform jazz" as a means of conceptualizing some of trumpeter Bill Dixon's solo pieces. The term itself is loosely defined by Dewar and is best described as formal organization that does not employ cyclical structures. Playing solo lends an obvious advantage to any musician seeking to employ such a formal model, mainly because it removes the need to communicate with fellow performers. This is by no means to suggest that jazz musicians had not explored such models within group contexts. Indeed, the music recorded by groups led by Cecil Taylor and Ornette Coleman had demonstrated some of the potential routes out of a traditional approach to form.

As Dewar points out, during the 1960s there were an increasing number of appearances on record of unaccompanied solos in the context of recordings made by groups. An important example here is clarinetist Jimmy Guiffre's *Free Fall* (1963), which featured Paul Bley and bassist Steve Swallow. Guiffre's group was formulating new approaches to group communication in the context of the leader's compositions, while also avoiding many of the practices involved in song-form jazz. Bley was an important figure in this respect as one of the few pianists to have played with Coleman. On *Freefall* (1963), Guiffre recorded five clarinet solos, along with a series of duets and trios involving Bley and Swallow. Guiffre's music managed, by his own account, to polarize opinion among American audiences, and this particular group was fairly short-lived. Another significant example of solo playing on record was Eric Dolphy's famous rendition of "God Bless the Child," recorded on bass clarinet in 1963, also mentioned by Dewar.

One of the most significant motivations behind solo playing came from musicians of the Association for the Advancement of Creative Musicians (AACM), based in Chicago, which did much to develop the idea of the improvised solo as a means of artistic development. Saxophonist Anthony Braxton made an important solo album in 1968 entitled simply *For Alto*, sometimes cited as an example of this developing interest in solo playing. But Braxton's recording developed out of the aesthetic agenda of the AACM, as explained by Ronald Radano: "Muhal Richard Abrams expected all musicians in the association to perform at least one unaccompanied solo concert. Abrams believed the exercise would enhance the musicians' understanding of musical form by forcing them to create a coherent musical structure on the spot."[8] It is significant that the motivation behind this exercise was to encourage musicians to confront the issue of form. In the aftermath of musical developments of the 1960s, form had become one of the primary challenges for musicians, especially when playing solo. In Braxton's own words, there was another aspect to this that went beyond developing a musical ability: "Unfortunately, I would also bring to the experience a concept of a psychology and the concept of freedom that was consistent with the '60s synergies as well. And, back in that time period: 'Oh freedom, we want freedom, we want freedom.'"[9] This link between the politically and culturally charged notion of freedom and musical practice has been a major theme in much recent scholarship on jazz from this period.[10]

Perhaps most significantly, South African pianist Abdullah Ibrahim (Dollar Brand) had recorded some solo piano albums in Europe in the late 1960s. These included *African Piano,* which was recorded in Copenhagen in 1969 but released in 1973 on the JAPO label. JAPO originated from the same record shop as ECM, and for a time it served as something of a sister label. Doubtless, then, Eicher would have been well aware of these records. The musical similarities between Ibrahim's approach and that of Jarrett were also considerable, not least because of Ibrahim's fondness for groove-driven compositions, which would segue one to another. Eicher would also surely have been aware that Joachim-Ernst Berendt liked to program solo pianists as part of some of the high-profile events he was involved with.[11] Eicher's own interest in recording solo musicians then emerged from a context in which there was already a considerable amount of activity in this field.

The Eicher-produced recordings by Corea, Bley, and Jarrett were among the earliest releases on ECM, and for parts of the American jazz press they came to define what the label was about. It is certainly possible to argue that the effect of the recordings went beyond simply promoting the image of ECM in America, to encouraging a wider take-up of solo piano performance. The 1973 Newport Jazz Festival included a concert of unaccompanied pianists, which was extended at the 1974 festival into two concerts, one featuring pianists who might have been considered traditional or mainstream (Teddy Wilson, Eubie Blake, Jess

Stacy, and Marian McPartland) and the other pianists who would have been considered part of a modern school (Bill Evans, Jarrett, McCoy Tyner, and Herbie Hancock). In the *New York Times*, John S. Wilson noted of the 1974 concert that it was considered "adventurous and daring" for the time, although he considered that Jarrett, Tyner, and Hancock "worked largely for mood effects."[12] The event was reported in the German *Jazz Podium* magazine as well, emphasizing the degree to which German fans could be kept abreast of developments on the American scene. The way in which it was reported makes clear that the German press was keenly aware of what constituted a modern school of jazz piano. The reviewer noted that the first concert emphasized the swing style but lacked the "current stage of development," while the Jarrett/Tyner/Hancock performance "demonstrated what is happening today on the 88 keys."[13] The Newport performance took place only a short time after the ECM releases became available in America. All three records appeared in America in 1972, but ECM's distribution system early on was limited. The Bley record was reviewed by *Down Beat* in October 1973, and the magazine then revisited the Jarrett and Bley recordings in 1975, reviewer Jon Balleras explaining to readers that, because of the improved distribution deal ECM had struck with Polydor, these records deserved to be reevaluated since they had become widely available.[14] On this basis, the case for regarding the Newport performances as a response to these records coming from Germany seems rather weak, given the time it took before the ECM releases were widely available.

The fact that the Corea, Bley, and Jarrett albums seem to have been singled out as a set can appear somewhat strange if based on perusal of ECM's discography. Though the records were all recorded around the same time, so was the Ralph Towner record *Diary* (1974), a solo album employing overdubbing techniques. And in 1972 Towner recorded *Trios/Solos* (1973), an album release under the names of Ralph Towner and Glen Moore. Eicher recorded the American pianist Steve Kuhn in 1974, producing his solo record *Ecstasy* (1975). Kuhn was perhaps most famous for the time he spent with John Coltrane, although Coltrane had replaced him with Tyner. Kuhn subsequently performed some solo dates in Europe, including a performance in Freiburg, Germany, alongside Towner's group Oregon, where *Jazz Podium* reported him playing a thirty-four-minute improvisation.[15] Kuhn had been living in Stockholm since 1967 and playing extensively throughout Europe, before returning to America in 1971. Another American pianist,

Richie Beirach would make the solo record *Hubris* (1978) for ECM. Yet Kuhn, Beirach, and Towner tend to be rather overlooked, perhaps in part because both the Kuhn and Beirach records remain extremely hard to find.[16] Furthermore, one can find other pianists not recording for ECM who made significant recordings at this time. Among them is the German pianist Joachim Kühn, whose album *Piano Solo* was recorded for MPS/BASF in 1972. In many respects, then, the idea of the Jarrett/Bley/Corea recordings as a set does not stand up in discographic terms.

However we group recordings together, it is undeniable that by the mid-1970s the solo piano record was suddenly an established part of jazz. As well as the pianists I have already mentioned, others who recorded solo in the wake of these ECM releases included McPartland (*Solo Concert at Haverford*, 1974), Andrew Hill (*Hommage*, 1975), Mary Lou Williams (*Solo Recital*, 1978), and Jimmy Rowles (*Jazz Is a Fleeting Moment*, 1975). There are also more indications of a general acceptance of solo playing. In a piece in the *Music Educator's Journal* in 1976, Ron Welburn wrote that performing in jazz unaccompanied was no longer unusual, citing Anthony Braxton, along with a roster of other musicians including Jarrett, Bley, and Corea.[17]

ECM SOLO SESSIONS: PIANO IMPROVISATIONS

Manfred Eicher seems to have been on something of a mission to recruit players to record solo for him in the early 1970s. Paul Bley describes how, when Eicher asked him to record solo, "it was one of a number of such calls he was putting out to his pianists."[18] Similarly, Annette Peacock recounts how Eicher asked her to record solo in 1970.[19] In describing the records Bley, Corea, and Jarrett made, Eicher noted how for all of the players "these recording sessions were their own discovery as well."[20] There is a sense that Eicher, as well as the pianists involved in recording for him, was setting out to make records that were not simply collections of standard tunes, and that there was a kind of artistic agenda involved. Corea described how:

> I met Manfred somewhere in Europe and he proposed the idea of a piano solo album.... And I was beginning, at that time, to experiment with more improvisation, more and more making up the form of the music as I went along. It seemed to be a good moment to go into the studio and try and lay down some of that thing. I remember Manfred

and I actually travelled around to a couple of solo concerts that I did in Germany around that time.[21]

For Corea and also for Jarrett, the opportunity to record allowed them to attempt something quite specific: sets of improvised miniatures that moved beyond conventional song forms. Although the title of the Corea albums (*Piano Improvisations*) might indicate otherwise, the majority of the pieces on the recordings do not seem to be free improvisations. The key perhaps is Corea's comment about making up the form. But what might that mean in practice, and is it a common theme across all three records?

The Jarrett and Corea albums consist almost entirely of original compositions (although Corea's *Piano Improvisations Vol. 2* includes "Trinkle Tinkle" by Thelonious Monk and "Masquelaro" by Wayne Shorter). One of the compositions on *Facing You*, "Vapallia," would later be recorded by Jarrett's American quartet on the 1974 album *Backhand*. Bley's recording has a slightly different emphasis in that, of the pieces on the record, three are by Carla Bley, two by Annette Peacock, and two by Bley himself. Some of the tunes on *Open, To Love* had previously appeared on other Bley recordings ("Closer" and "Ida Lupino" both appear on the 1965 album *Closer*). So Bley seems to have been working with a fair amount of extant material in the studio, a slightly different approach from that taken by either Jarrett or Corea.

On all three recordings, there are a number of pieces that use conventional form, i.e., a cyclical structure with a fixed harmonic and metric framework, which is the standard approach to form within postbop jazz. On Jarrett's *Facing You*, both "Starbright" and "Semblance" use cyclical structures, which are fairly easy to hear. In the case of "Starbright," the form is a twenty-bar head, after which Jarrett improvises over an eight-bar harmonic cycle. "Semblance" is a twelve-bar form, although harmonically it is a long way from a blues sequence. Indeed, "Semblance" made its way into the illegal version of *The Real Book* that is taken to have originated at the Berklee College of Music in Boston during the 1970s. In total, then, of the eight tunes on *Facing You*, three are based on cyclical structures.

Corea's recordings also contained a number of tunes with cyclical structures. The second track from *Piano Improvisations Vol. 1*, "Song for Sally," sets up an alternation between a sixteen-bar vamp section in A minor, with a twelve-bar bridge that moves downwards from A minor to the dominant, E, before recapitulating the A section. "Song of the Wind" works with a long, repeated harmonic sequence in waltz time after a free introduction. However, it is in the other pieces on both the Jarrett and Corea records that we find the most significant approach to form.

DEFINING FORM IN JAZZ

Jazz musicians use the term *form* to mean something quite specific, as jazz scholar Robert Hodson points out.[22] Form is used to mean the structure of a tune, that is the underlying harmonic and metric framework of the compositions used as the basis for performance. Barry Kernfeld describes form in his book *What to Listen for in Jazz* as follows: "Jazz forms are simple and, in a way, unimportant.... Once a form is identified, a listener's attention turns elsewhere. Forms are the least significant building blocks of jazz."[23] Kernfeld sees form as no more than the mold into which music is poured. His view is conceived with relation to a kind of common practice in postbop jazz where forms are dictated by the compositions musicians choose to play. In this practice, soloists and rhythm sections follow the chorus structure of the tune, demarcating it carefully while often even marking the individual subsections of the form (every eight bars in the case of the thirty-two-bar song form), playing improvisations over the chord changes. But it is also clear that, viewed from this perspective, form can be a constraint, not merely an organizational feature. In purely theoretical terms, it is possible to argue that, if improvisers have to follow the chord changes in their playing, then soloing is no more than a complex painting-by-numbers exercise. Of course few jazz musicians would see it this way; nonetheless at various times the formal structures of the standard jazz repertoire have been seen by some as limiting musical invention, imposing restrictions on how musicians can express themselves.

At the same time, there is a powerful and important stream of development in jazz that has negotiated flexibilities that can be created within this context, in an attempt to avoid the straitjacketing effect form can have. It was perhaps inevitable that jazz musicians would, at some point, either reject or significantly refine the bebop model of performance, in which the form of the composition exerted such a controlling influence. That moment has usually been seen as the free jazz movement of the 1960s, represented by the appearance of Ornette Coleman on the New York jazz scene in 1959.

The idea of freedom that Coleman's music espoused was a powerful one. At a stroke, it seemed to allow musicians freedoms within the context of compositions that seemed unthinkable to some. Yet as Eric Charry demonstrates, the reality is that Coleman's music was far from formless; it was rather that his compositions did not operate conventionally in terms of the relationship between musician and form.[24] The narrative surrounding Coleman's music is a good example of what Robert Hodson has called a "negative" definition of free jazz: it is defined in terms of what it lacks in relation to what was standard practice at the time.[25] Hodson suggests that what is generally described in relation to free jazz is a situation where, instead of form determining a set of constraints that musicians have to deal with *in* performance, these constraints and musical materials are a result *of* performance. Yet Charry's work, and the substantial literature in this area, demonstrates that this music is far from formless. The extreme of formlessness understood as the absence of any compositional organization was one that was really approached only through free improvisation, a tradition developed most notably in Europe. Indeed many free improvisers treat jazz with suspicion because of its reliance on form and procedure, or what the guitarist and writer on the subject Derek Bailey would have called the "idiomatic."[26]

For much of the 1960s, even though the aesthetic of freedom was important, it never (or at least rarely) prompted the complete jettisoning of compositional form. We can find musicians still concerned with playing standard song forms, but reconceptualizing those forms and their influence while performing. Miles Davis and Sonny Rollins are perhaps two of the best examples of this tendency. Rollins, as on the extraordinary *Sonny Meets Hawk* album (1963), demonstrated an approach to playing over the changes obviously influenced by the avant-garde, set against a rhythm section that delineates the form of the tunes very clearly. Rollins then wanted the form, while at the same time finding ways of playing more "out" or freely over that form.

In the case of the Davis group, with Herbie Hancock, Wayne Shorter, Ron Carter, and Tony Williams, this exploration began to alter the form of the tune itself, substituting different chords and rhythmic feels, moving from one tempo to another. The skeleton of the form remains, but its gradual reshaping in performance was brilliantly documented on recordings such as *My Funny Valentine* (1965).[27] A more radical approach is usually associated with free jazz and with musicians such as John Coltrane and Albert Ayler. But as is well documented, Coltrane's extended playing developed in the context of playing tunes, either his own compositions or versions of standard tunes (a notable example being "My Favorite Things"). Even in his later work, such as *Interstellar Space* (1967) and *Ascension* (1965), there are organizational elements at work, be they vamps, modal areas, or themes. These elements may not be organized conventionally into a compositional form as might be expected for post-bop jazz, but they retain some key organizational elements.

Hodson has provided a framework for understanding how form might function in a range of examples that could be called precursors to free jazz.[28] His examination of tracks by Evans, Davis, and Coleman demonstrates how musicians interact with elements of form. Rather than form determining the materials of performance, as it might be said to do in the postbop model, musicians can now interact with the form in certain ways. In the case of Davis's "Flamenco Sketches" from *Kind of Blue* (1959), though the harmonic progression used is determined compositionally, the musicians can shape the proportion of time spent in each modal area in performance, so that the resulting structure is not defined by the form of the composition. This is an important theoretical understanding, because it provides an alternative to the formlessness that has been one of the standard, but unhelpful, descriptions of free jazz. It is true that many musicians dealt with the question of form in their own way. The kind of plurality in free jazz that Ekkehard Jost describes has often been used as a way of emphasizing the appetite for innovation that many musicians had, but the impression one gets is of a variety of approaches.[29] As I will demonstrate in the next section, in this light the recordings by Jarrett, Bley, and Corea can all be seen in terms of a particular kind of approach to form. In this one respect they are remarkably consistent and demonstrate a distinctive post-1960s approach, one that is important in understanding *The Köln Concert*.

COREA'S "NOON SONG"

"Noon Song" is the first track from Corea's *Piano Improvisations Vol. 1*, and the kind of formal template it suggests is one that proves useful in considering the rest of the music from both Corea's and Jarrett's recordings. Corea begins the piece with a long, rhapsodic melody in the right hand, over a left-hand part that outlines in broken chord formation a rich D major sonority (with added sixth and ninth). This opening statement proceeds through a sequence of harmonies as follows: $D^{6/9}$–$F^{\#13}$–Bm^7 (Bm^6)–A^{13}–$D^{6/9}$. This first paragraph of music thus outlines a simple I-III-vi-V-I progression. The manner in which this opening is played is not arrhythmic, but the sense of pulse behind the music is subtle, Corea's cascading right-hand lines seeming to float over a subtly inferred beat. This first paragraph defines not the form of the piece but the material from which Corea's improvisation takes its cue. It establishes a harmonic area and chord sequence, but crucially here the music is without definite meter. The opening statement, then, is more like a blueprint than a "head."

Corea proceeds neither by adhering to this harmonic cycle, nor departing from it entirely. In what follows, the music still progresses as it does at the outset from D major to the $F^{\#13}$ secondary dominant chord, but in the second iteration Corea then moves onto an F major harmony, and then back up to $F^{\#}$ after a few seconds. Here the harmonic cycle is being reworked, but not radically because its overall shape is retained. This is not a chord substitution, replacing one chord with another, because in this statement the $F^{\#}$ harmony lasts for longer than previously because of the interjection of the F major chord. In this way successive statements rework the harmonic cycle, doing more than substituting or altering chords: in effect actually modifying the sequence. Also, each harmony is not fixed to a metrical structure. Each statement can expand or contract, in this case becoming longer than the previous, while the harmonic template remains ever present in the background.

In some respects, this may seem like a classical theme-and-variations format, in that it moves from a simple statement of a theme to increasingly complex variations of that material. The variations between statements, however, function not merely as a means of decorating harmonic and melodic structures but actually manipulate the original outline such that it expands and contracts at Corea's whim. This kind of formal approach might be what Corea meant when he talked of making up the form while playing. This way of approaching form is much more fluid and flexible than the typical jazz conception of metrically fixed cyclical structures, but neither is the result entirely open. Having looked at one example from Corea's recording, I now want to turn to two short examples from Jarrett's *Facing You.*

JARRETT'S "LALENE"

Unlike "Noon Song," Jarrett's "Lalene" begins in a way that appears unambiguous. As seen in Example 3.1, the left hand sets up a bass note and chord pattern.[30] Although this may look highly syncopated on paper, the sonic result actually sounds quite regular. Because of a subtle use of the pedal, these syncopations are not rhythmically emphasized. There is also what seems to be a clear metrical structure. The harmony moves at a largely predictable and regular pace, generally one chord to a bar or half bar. This kind of regular motion usually signifies a composition in jazz, given that such metrically predictable harmonic motion is typical of jazz standards. As a result, the piece starts sounding very much like the others on the record that use conventional cyclical forms, such as "Starbright." However, "Lalene" does not display a conventional formal model.

The opening phrase of the piece begins on an E major chord, but with a distinctive Lydian sharpened fourth in the melody, cadencing on to B major at the end of the fourth bar as shown in Example 3.1. Melodically, this opening segment splits into two distinct, but clearly identifiable, phrases. The first phrase is followed by another of four bars' length, which, again, begins on E major but ends this time on an uncertain E/F# chord. Indeed the phrasing during the first minute of music strongly implies a sixteen-bar structure. Although this gives the impression that there is likely to be a regular form to the piece based on a cyclical framework, this is not so. For the first couple of minutes, the harmony inhabits an area defined by the opening, moving around a group of chords including B major, F#, G#, D# minor, and E, with occasional moves to more distant chords. Yet these harmonies are not connected by any one repeated progression; rather Jarrett moves between them quite freely.

It is possible to discern in the piece one underlying thread running throughout: the occasional return to a particular chord progression. In its first iteration the progression is E^{maj9}–$G^#$–$C^#m^9$. This progression recurs in a number of places, but every time what follows is slightly different. As the piece proceeds, the length of time between statements of the progression increases. The music becomes ever more adventurous during the middle of the piece, developing into fast, weaving right-hand lines. Yet after these long episodes, Jarrett returns to this progression, such as at 6'14" after a particularly long passage. Here he works the progression through three times, following it with a brief

EXAMPLE 3.1   Opening of "Lalene"

recapitulation of some of the opening melodic material at 7'15" before a short coda.

"Lalene" is certainly not a formless or free piece, but at the same time it does not employ any of the usual formal archetypes we might expect in jazz. Jarrett sets out with a thematic idea, and even if he returns to one particular harmonic thread throughout, what occurs between these iterations seems to be constrained in no way by the material stated at the outset. Corea's "Ballad for Anna" from *Piano Improvisations Vol. 1* works in a strikingly similar way, moving through a series of related harmonies, while never seeming to exactly repeat exactly any one progression.

But what kind of form is this? In "Noon Song" I suggested that Corea began with a single harmonic progression, which was then segmented and expanded as the piece went on. The material that defined the form was established from the start. The same, I would suggest, is true here, except that the organization of the piece does not establish any one sequence for these harmonies. As we will see with the next example, this kind of formal architecture contains what are effectively vestiges of cyclical progressions. But it also hints at a new way of conceptualizing improvisations in the context of thematic material.

JARRETT'S "IN FRONT"

"In Front" is possibly the most important piece on *Facing You*. It is the track that begins the album, but it is also the longest. In many respects this single track is most central to understanding how Jarrett came to deal with form in his solo concert performances, such as that of *The Köln Concert*.

"In Front" begins with a very clear thematic idea, with a tenor voice moving underneath right-hand chords answered by a line moving into the upper part of the right hand (Example 3.2).[31] Unlike "Lalene," in this excerpt the sense of pulse is very hard to pin down. This is partly because at the outset the pulse is more clearly articulated in the left hand than in the right, so the combination of the two hands creates a rather ambiguous rhythmic feel. This kind of approach can be found in much of Jarrett's music with his trio of the time, with Charlie Haden and Paul Motian, and is often traced back to Ornette Coleman. Indeed one can find a similar kind of feel emerging in some of Coleman's recordings from the late 1950s, such as the famous "Lonely Woman" from *The Shape of Jazz to Come* (1959).[32] At the start of "In Front" Jarrett plays the motif I have shown (see Example 3.2), stating it three times. What happens during the

EXAMPLE 3.2   Opening of "In Front"

rest of the piece is indicated in Table 3.1, which is a sketch of the overall organization.

The conception "In Front" demonstrates is a simple but powerful one. Rather than the form of the piece being dictated by the composition, or in this case by the precomposed material, instead the form can emerge from those elements in the course of the performance. The elements can be combined in different ways, and expanded or contracted as the performer sees fit. This can be seen very clearly from the way Jarrett treats the opening. The initial statement is clearly demarcated, as is obvious from the manner in which it is repeated exactly. That repetition signals the motivic status of the material and signifies composition. This motive returns after a series of "excursions," passages that are not bound harmonically by the motivic material in the way that improvisations over a song form would normally be. Jarrett retains an awareness of the tonal area in which he is working, moving away gradually in order to return; at the same time these excursions develop and expand, such that the motivic material recedes into the distance. A new musical area emerges as Jarrett moves toward an F pedal, which then develops into a vamp passage on F. At the close of the piece, when the initial melodic material returns, the music has moved through three or four contrasting musical episodes. These contrasts are not merely surface decorations, nice ways of disguising similar musical material; rather, each in its own right functions almost as an autonomous entity, with its own forms of organization, harmonic characteristics, and so on.

TABLE 3.1   Organization of "In Front"

0'00"	*Theme (x3)*	
0'30"	Excursion 1	Harmony begins to move chromatically up from F, settling finally onto Bb
0'51"	Theme (x1)	
1'00"	Excursion 2	Begins with a bluesy figure in F, before moving off harmonically, only to return to F again before the next iteration of the theme
1'37"	Theme (x1)	
1'45"	Excursion 3	Begins by moving upward chromatically again, but remains harmonically unsettled
2'31"	Theme (x1)	Slightly modified
2'40"	Excursion 4	Long blues vamp passage on F
6'11"		Slightly slower, moving harmonically
7'45"		Settles into quieter, slower, ballad-type music, more harmonically ambiguous
8'45"	Theme (x2)	Much slower than the outset, and reharmonized the second time
9'30"–10'02"	Coda	

Taken together then, what do these examples from the Corea and Jarrett albums say about form? Both records contain a number of pieces with conventional cyclical forms, suggesting that the musicians were not entirely rejecting the postbop model of song form, and indeed were quite happy to work within that model. At the same time, many of the pieces on the albums suggested a new relationship between improviser and form, and a new way of conceptualizing composition. In all of the pieces, there are clearly compositional elements brought to the music by the performers, and those elements help define the parameters within which the music is created. So, for instance, it might be the opening idea in Jarrett's "In Front" that acts as a thematic and gestural point of return, after increasingly complex improvised excursions. Or it might be Corea's template in "Noon Song" that becomes ever more expanded and varied as the piece progresses. In the summary I presented earlier, I began from the jazz musicians' conception of form, as a kind of invariant harmonic-metrical structure, almost like a map showing a route from A to B. The form of a piece, seen this way, applies a constraining influence on the musician, harmonically, rhythmically, and structurally. But rather than seeing form as a guiding principle that involves a bundling together of these musical parameters, it is possible to imagine that form could mean a musician being constrained only harmonically, or only metrically.

In the pieces I have discussed performers have come up with organizational schemes that give them certain constraints within which to work: the harmonic sequence in Corea's "Noon Song," the thematic fragment for the theme-and-variations-type structure in "In Front," and the harmonic sequences that act as a point of return in "Lalene." As we will see shortly, this kind of conception of form is enormously important for understanding the music of Jarrett's solo concert recordings, and *The Köln Conc*ert in particular.

CHAPTER 4

ONE OF THE CENTRAL appeals of *The Köln Concert* recording is that it documents a piece of improvised music, created in one fleeting moment in a German concert hall in 1975. It is the fixing of that performance in sonic form that allows it to be listened to repeatedly and studied. But a recording is not the same thing as a score produced by a composer, the objects most usually subjected to music analysis. The Cologne performance exists only in sound, not as notes on a page (although a transcription does exist, as I will discuss in the next chapter). This is not just a difference in format because, although a score is open to a range of interpretations and realizations, Jarrett's performance has only one real form, that of the recording. The recording is not the same thing as the performance, but the result of a series of technological and artistic mediations. Some musicians have made arrangements of the Cologne improvisations, but those are different things altogether, not recreations of the performance but imitations or reinterpretations. A recording of an improvised piece is qualitatively different from a notated composition. Whereas a composer can choose to craft a piece in a variety of ways, not working in a linear fashion but shaping segments one at a time, and revising previously written material, an improviser is locked into a temporality in which material cannot be revised once it is played.[1] But what might any of this mean for analysis of improvised music?

JAZZ RECORDINGS AS INTERTEXTS

In the introduction to his book *Free Jazz*, Ekkehard Jost states that analyzing a jazz musician's improvisations "demands that the analyst take into account everything he has learned from *other* improvisations by the same musician."[2] Jost quotes Gunther Schuller's suggestion that the improvisations of a musician, "form a chain of non-definitive phenomena."[3] In other words, no improvisation can be truly complete or self-contained; it is instead part of an ongoing process.

It is tempting to think that improvisers function in a creative vacuum, that things really do come off the top of the head and happen only once. And it is nice to think this way because it allows us, when we go to hear a jazz performance, to feel we are witnessing something special, which will never be repeated. Yet what most of us do not see are the daily preparations and rituals that inform the way any musician plays: the practicing, rehearsing, warming up, and so on. The literature on improvisation that has emerged over the last decade or more provides a nuanced understanding of the degree to which improvisation is a practiced, learned art.[4] Musicians work night after night on their improvisations, developing a set of devices and strategies; not necessarily repeating themselves literally, but working with the elements of a personal language.

Following Gunther Schuller's comment about improvisations forming part of a chain, we can see how recordings might serve to document works in progress. The improviser who reworks ideas time after time may or may not be in search of the perfect solo, but this process will continue throughout the whole of a career. In the event, each recording is an incomplete and imperfect document of a performance that is part of a chain compiled over a musician's lifetime, the totality of which is too much for any recording to capture. Yet this view runs contrary to the tendency to treat sound recordings as autonomous texts.

One of the implications of viewing recordings as part of an ongoing chain of connected performances is that they are essentially intertextual. Intertextuality, an idea famously articulated by Julia Kristeva, posits that texts are related to one another and do not stand as independent entities.[5]

The term *text* takes the place of "work" in such theoretical discourse to signal a difference between the idea of a work as an autonomous, closed object possessing a single stable meaning and a text possessing multiple meanings (by definition more fluid). The concept of intertextuality is used by some musicologists as a means of commenting on how one work, or text, quotes from, or comments on, another. But intertextuality is an idea that has far more radical implications, because it does not simply examine relationships between texts but rather rethinks the whole idea of what constitutes a text's identity and meaning. To see a text as "radically plural," as Graham Allen suggests, means not simply looking within for meaning but tracing that text's formation across a range of contexts.[6]

In the case of popular music recordings, Serge Lacasse has explored some applications of intertextuality, via a transposition of this theory to phonography, a terminology first used by Evan Eisenberg in *The Recording Angel*.[7] So what kind of formation of intertext or interphonography might we apply to the case of Jarrett? As I have already established, Jarrett would undertake solo concert tours where he usually performed every other day, sometimes on consecutive nights. This kind of itinerary would give little time for him to rid himself of the memory of the previous performance. The fact that in an interview with journalist Peter Ruedi Jarrett alluded to listening to the tape of the Cologne performance just days after the concert also confirms that there was sometimes a process of reviewing recorded performances while on tour.[8] Naturally enough, then, it makes sense to try to understand the music of the Cologne performance in relation to other performances from the same tour. Doing so is an exercise not in trying to spot repetition but rather about seeking to place the performance in a textual field. Of course, it would be possible to broaden this field almost endlessly, to take in all of Jarrett's other performances and recordings that year—or further, to include his entire career. Any such comparisons would be valid, even if the weight of material involved might prove rather cumbersome. Here I will deliberately focus attention on the January and February 1975 performances, after some further discussion of the issue of form.

FORM IN IMPROVISED MUSIC

I have suggested that in the recordings Jarrett and Chick Corea made for ECM in the early 1970s, we find a new way of dealing with form. But how might we understand form in regard to Jarrett's solo concert improvisations, which set out to be something different from the miniatures of *Facing You*? Is form simply the end result, the shape that the music takes on as it is played, or is form a kind of organizing force that mediates in the course of the improvisation? As I suggested in the preceding chapter, accounts of free jazz or free improvisation often rely on negative definitions, describing music through the absence of form. This situation reflects not only a critical failure to deal with a substantial amount of jazz and improvised music but also the fact that the study of such music is often difficult. The song forms used by jazz musicians playing a mainstream postbop repertoire served analysts well, because they supported a fairly simple correlation between what jazz musicians played and the underlying form from which they were working. It is in this light that musicologist Nicholas Cook describes how improvisation has usually been thought of as "relational."[9] But what alternative is there when the music under examination appears to forgo all compositional organization?

In a 1984 article, Jeff Pressing argues that improvisation across artistic traditions can be understood in terms of the employment of a "referent", which is "used to facilitate the generation and edition of improvised behavior on an intermediate time scale."[10] Pressing suggests that a referent can take a host of forms depending on the context, from a highly formal scheme to an abstract idea governing behavior. In writing of free jazz, he comments that it has "normally no referent, although sometimes a very loosely structured out-of-time one is used, not based on traditional tonal musical structures."[11] The general thrust of Pressing's theory is that there can be a variety of kinds of organization used to generate improvisations. As I argued in the previous chapter, Jarrett's *Facing You* suggests that the forms of organization being deployed in and through improvisation range greatly from one piece to another, and even sometimes within a piece. One section may have a clear harmonic organization, another may have a metric/rhythmic structure but lack an easily definable harmonic scheme, and so on. What this suggests is that it might be better to understand the strategies improvisers employ in terms of musical parameters, rather than as single guiding principles.

Gernot Blume's 1998 dissertation on Jarrett paved the way for a number of subsequent writers.[12] Blume was keen to identify Jarrett as a musician who drew from differing musical traditions, incorporating their influence into his own language. This approach established that Jarrett's style of playing developed through his encounters with various musics. This helps to explain how his language is significantly different from that of most free improvisers. Free improvisation, as opposed to free jazz, developed particularly through the work of European musicians wanting to emancipate themselves from what were sometimes seen as the constraints of the jazz tradition, seeking a freedom from cliché and the idiomatic, in Derek Bailey's words.[13] This was an attempt to escape the standard language that jazz musicians used, in order to forge an entirely new one. In this respect, Jarrett stands quite apart from many free improvisers because, for the most part, his improvisations do not seek this distance from the jazz language. Instead they work within that language, extending it into other stylistic areas, thus creating a sense of familiarity for the listener.

In a 2003 article, Blume outlines simply a view of Jarrett's playing style that offers the potential for a range of analytical inquiries: "Jarrett creates a set of repeatable procedures and formulaic practices that reinstate the effects of idiomatic delineation. He forges a style out of his melange of styles to communicate with his audiences in an identifiable conceptual framework. His language appears original by interweaving conventions that belong to a number of musical systems and traditions."[14] Blume devotes some attention to the first part of the Cologne concert, segmenting the opening improvisation using terms such as "Intro," "Groove 1," "Rubato 1," "Slow Rubato," and so on.[15] This labeling strategy is based on the foregrounding of rhythmic aspects, creating an understanding of the improvisation in terms of what he sees as a sense of energy or intensity. Of course this kind of labeling could just as easily be undertaken using harmonic criteria. The characteristics that Blume defines are paralleled by other musical parameters; indeed these characteristics might be said to cluster together to form what could be called "style."

Many critics and musicologists have heard a series of particular stylistic references in Jarrett's improvisations. I have argued elsewhere that these are not mere passing references to different musics; they can be understood as styles Jarrett employs in the course of his improvisations, styles that form part of a commonly understood musical language.[16] Each style can be described in terms of a set of musical criteria, or what we might call a set of constraints—musical parameters that govern how Jarrett improvises. One approach to analyzing these improvisations is to attempt to identify what these organizing factors are, and consider making a kind of formal segmentation based on how they are manifest in the improvisations. In order to demonstrate a little of how this works, and how each Jarrett improvisation has to be considered as part of a larger textual field, I will spend a little time discussing groove passages.

GROOVE PASSAGES

Groove passages are perhaps one of the most identifiable elements of Jarrett's solo playing style. The main characteristic of these passages is the use of left-hand vamp patterns to generate a groove and outline a harmonic context. Groove passages can be found as far back as Jarrett's early recordings with Charles Lloyd, as well as in his most recent solo work.[17] They are, in short, a remarkably consistent part of his musical vocabulary. His first solo recordings for ECM certainly exhibit plenty of examples, such as a number of passages on the *Solo Concerts* (1973) recording, and part of "In Front" from *Facing You* (1971). Jarrett used similar kinds of templates for a number of the pieces he recorded with his groups. The *Belonging* record, made in 1974, included the tune "Long As You Know You're Living Yours," essentially a groove piece driven by piano, bass, and drums vamping. Tracing the lineage of these groove passages back through Jarrett's music is only one part of the story. They can also be placed as part of a broader tradition of using harmonically static grooves and vamps as the basis for improvisation, an idea that extended its influence beyond jazz into some forms of rock music during the middle to late 1960s.

I will discuss the groove passages in the Cologne concert in some detail in Chapters Five and Six. But here I am interested in considering the types of groove passage we find in the performances from the 1975 tour. The first example I want to discuss here is what I will term a blues vamp. This particular instance comes seventeen minutes into the first part of the Kronach performance, from January 17, 1975. As shown in Example 4.1, the passage works with three chords set into the vamp: a G major chord that drops quickly to F major and then down to C. The vamp itself maintains a rhythmic momentum generated in part by Jarrett's left hand, which rocks between root notes an octave apart, coupled with the rhythmically charged chords in the right hand. There is an inner part providing a little harmonic filler, played usually with the first two fingers of the right hand, or on occasion the thumb of the left hand. Jarrett plays this passage without any pedal, and with a strong rhythmic articulation. These characteristics define the groove quality of the passage. The blues inflection comes through the use of the ♭VII chord (F major) in the context of a G major tonality, as well the use of "crushed" notes such as the B♭/B in the sixth bar of the example. Although the music of this passage is not strictly speaking a blues in formal terms, it retains the harmonic characteristics that evoke the blues, while harnessing a groove rhythmically.

In the case of a groove passage such as this, the main function of the figuration is to establish a rhythmic and harmonic template. Jarrett groove passages often begin by establishing this figuration before he proceeds to improvise right-hand lines over the groove maintained by the

EXAMPLE 4.1   Blues vamp from Kronach Concert, Part 1, 17'20"

left hand. In this sense such passages function almost like the soloist–rhythm section split in the jazz ensemble. Jarrett's left hand and chordal filler maintain the groove and harmony, with the right hand acting as the soloist. One of the results of using a repetitive groove like this is that difference becomes particularly marked. Repetition serves to create a forward-directed expectation of further repetition, and therefore any deviation from expectation becomes particularly heightened. Jarrett exploits this by inserting break-downs into vamp passages, pausing to modulate through a number of keys before returning to the vamp. But again, as we will see in the coming chapters, the idea of musically generated expectations is particularly important when considering the expressive effect these improvisations create.

Although the Cologne performance employs a number of vamp passages, none of them begins as a blues vamp in quite the way this particular passage does. A blues vamp is just one of a number of groove passage types Jarrett employs, differentiated usually by their harmonic approach. My designation of blues inflection is based on specific harmonic devices: use of dominant seventh harmony, ^{b}VII chords, and crushed blue notes. However, there are many groove passages in the improvisations that use vamps but do not have these blues inflections. There are, for example, one-chord vamps where the harmony does not change. These vamps can be minor key, sometimes using a mode like the Phrygian, which provides a particular harmonic hue. Take for instance a passage (Example 4.2) from around eleven minutes in to the first improvisation from the Bremen concert of February 2, 1975. Here the harmonic context of

EXAMPLE 4.2   Vamp from Bremen Concert, Part 1, 11'44"

the vamp is quite different. The harmony is based on an E^b drone sustained in the left hand, with a Eb major sonority above. However this chord is also inflected with a very foreign-sounding flattened sixth degree (C^b), emphasized strongly in the second bar of this excerpt through a series of trill-like gestures. In this instance the vamp is harmonically static.

If this is a major key vamp inflected with an Aeolian-sounding flattened sixth, there are also vamps built on uninflected major key harmonies, a number of which occur in the Cologne performance. And then there are minor key vamps, which appear at the start of some of the improvisations from the 1975 tour. The Freiburg, Paris, and Evergreen College concerts all open with minor-key vamp passages. This is not to suggest that Jarrett is recycling material, and comparison of the passages in question reveals anything but, as shown in Example 4.3.

It will be immediately apparent that these differing instances from performances separated by more than ten days are not obviously connected, at least from the notation. However, they are unquestionably all of the same type. They all generate rhythmic momentum in the form of a groove in the left hand, although in the example from the Paris concert the right hand is particularly important in the way that it interlocks with the left. Although these are all minor-key vamps, harmony is not articulated in a conventional triadic fashion, as it is with the Bremen vamp in Example 4.2. Rather, these vamps are built from quartal harmony, that is, with the use of fourths. In the case of the Freiburg passage, this is clearly demonstrated by the sustained right-hand chord and the way the left hand outlines the same pitch pattern built on fourths: C-F-B^b. With the Paris example the harmony is articulated in closely positioned chords, with these fourths truncated into a smaller pitch space, while in the Evergreen College example the right hand plays bare fourths and fifths over the left-hand vamp. Here we have three passages in different keys, from three performances, that share the same underlying textural and harmonic construction. Plainly they are all built from a common blueprint

EXAMPLE 4.3 Minor Key Vamps from 1975 Concerts

Freiburg, January 21, 1975

♩=126

Paris, February 5, 1975

♩=124

Evergreen College, February 20, 1975

♩=102

that defines the role of the left hand and the construction of the harmony. The sample I use here includes only vamps from the start of
improvisations, and naturally the available recordings document only a
relatively small percentage of the music Jarrett performed during this
1975 tour. There is a good chance that across one concert tour Jarrett used
this particular kind of construction on many occasions. Naturally, this
sort of approach could be extended to categorizing the kinds of vamps
Jarrett employs during this 1975 tour, and identifying instances of each.

BALLAD PASSAGES

Although groove passages rely on harmonic stasis and a highly regular-
ized repetitive framework, there are many other passages in Jarrett improvisations that, by contrast, are far more harmonically mobile. One
type I have discussed elsewhere is the ballad passage.[18] Example 4.4
shows the opening of the Bremen concert from February 2, 1975.

EXAMPLE 4.4   Opening of Bremen Concert

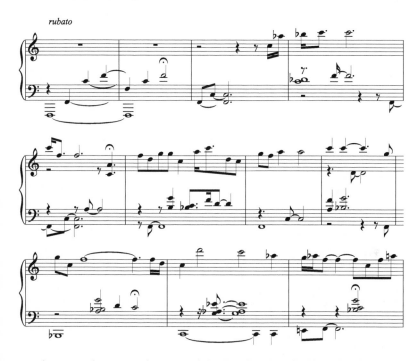

The music begins with an F pedal, articulated at the opening as a rum-
bling low register sonority, but there is a certain ambiguity over the diatonic area. The B^b minor inflection in bar 4 (which could be interpreted
as F Aeolian) gives way to F major, but the V-I cadence in bar 11 then
leads on to F minor. Stripped to its essence, this passage begins with
what could be described as a I-IV-V-I motion in F. But the interest comes
from the different ways in which these harmonies are inflected and
voiced, and the fact that there are relatively few places where there is an
unambiguous triadic harmony at work. The rate at which the harmony
changes is somewhat irregular, a sense reinforced by the rubato perme-
ating the music. The result is that there is no articulation of a regular
harmonic sequence, as there is in groove passages.

The music that follows from this example describes a further unfold-
ing. Rather than this I-IV-V-I progression forming a cyclical structure or
a kind of ground bass, the harmony expands to include other chords
from the implied tonal area. There is a clear sense of harmonic organization in this passage, but one not articulated through a cyclical structure
or a repeated harmony, in the way that happens with vamp passages.

Rather, it is predicated on the idea of moving through and around an established harmonic area, avoiding any metric regularity in terms of where the harmony changes.

The music of Example 4.4 is obviously more harmonically mobile than the previous passages I have described, but there are instances in the solo improvisations of considerably greater mobility. A useful account of how we might understand such music is provided by Steven Termini, in his 2006 thesis on Jarrett. Termini addresses the issue of how Jarrett is able to deal with moment-to-moment choices in improvisation. He identifies what he calls four "automata" Jarrett employs in his improvisations. One of the automata Termini describes is what he calls the "Jarrett Circle of Fifths."[19] Jazz musicians are very used to navigating chord progressions in which the root note moves by a fifth. The ii-V-I progression is one of the harmonic building blocks of most Tin Pan Alley songs, which are a staple of the jazz repertoire. A song such as Jerome Kern's "All the Things You Are" can be analyzed entirely in terms of ii-V-I progressions moving through various tonal centers. Termini suggests that Jarrett will often link circle-of-fifths progressions with stepwise bass movement or movement by a third. The effect is to promote a harmonic mobility that can accomplish movement between one tonal center and another very quickly, all through use of what sound like very conventional, localized chord changes.

The opening passage from the Kronach improvisation shown in Example 4.5 demonstrates something of what Termini means. Here, the motion between one harmony and another is accomplished through

EXAMPLE 4.5   Opening of Kronach Concert

bass motion by a fifth, stepwise, or a third. In this case the effect is an underlying sense of restlessness, created by the lack of any firm resolution within this passage. That is also a function of the harmonic construction, in which the harmony is not built triadically above the bass note but instead via a series of triads superimposed above. If notated, this would result in what are usually called "slash" chords, and the opening two harmonies could be interpreted as E^b/F and B^b/C. Here again, though, the harmonic effect is quite different from the stasis of a groove passage. The sense of expectation generated here relates to ongoing motion, quite the opposite of establishing an unambiguous harmonic center. In both of these examples, it is possible to discern an underlying set of musical principles common to the passages. But the next question must involve moving beyond identifying such types, to understanding their expressive function.

IMPROVISATION, RISK, AND TIME

In order to understand Jarrett's solo concert improvisations, it is useful to think of them as moving through a range of musical and expressive states. The move from one state to another, or from one kind of music to another, can in itself be expressive. In his study of Beethoven's late works, musicologist Robert Hatten invokes the idea of expressive genre. Expressive genres are, he says, "based on … [and] move through broad expressive states oppositionally defined as topics in the classical style."[20] So it is that an improvisation beginning in a ballad style and moving gradually into a groove passage could be said to employ a particular expressive genre. Not only can the ballad and groove styles be said to be based on blueprints that connect each instance, but their usage within an expressive progression comes to establish a higher-level pattern. This is an important understanding in this context, because what gives Jarrett's improvisations a sense of direction is how they move through a series of musical state changes, which can be described using Hatten's concept of expressive genre.

But what is this music expressive of? Put differently, how is it expressive? As I have already suggested, the cultural resonance of *The Köln Concert* rested in large part on the way it seemed to articulate an idea about music and music making. And this is a key factor in understanding the music's expressive potential. Consider for instance a comment made by Richard Williams in a review of a 1977 Jarrett solo performance, where he mentions "lengthy spells during which inspiration deserts him [Jarrett] and he merely toys with a simple vamp until a new idea arrives."[21] Williams has a particular interpretation of Jarrett's vamp passages: not only are they musically tedious but they signify something about the creative process, namely that the improviser has reached an impasse. Does this mean that every time Jarrett plays a repetitive vamp passage he is stuck? One would think not, given the regularity with which they occur in his improvisations. Is Williams hearing something specific to this performance, and how do we know whether or not he is right? The answer is that we do not and cannot know, unless the improviser tells us specifically afterward, and even then it is difficult to take his or her word for it.

Whether or not Williams and the many other critics who have heard Jarrett's groove passages this way are correct in their inference, such remarks indicate something important about how we listen to improvised music. When we listen, we are hearing not only the music but the improviser in the music. If Williams hears tedium because he is aware of listening to Jarrett creating music on the spot, so improvised music can be heard as a direct reflection of the creative process.

What motivates musicians who practice free improvisation? Jazz musicians have an enormous body of compositional material to fall back on, so it is not as if there is a need to generate completely new material in every performance. Musicians who set out to create performances without using any prepared material invoke risk, an aesthetic discussed by John Corbett in his 1994 book *Extended Play*. Corbett begins with what constitutes a standard kind of definition of improvisation: "Pat Question: How does an improviser improvise? Pat Answer: He or she develops and employs a repertoire of possibilities."[22] This is a deterministic view of improvisation in that improvisers must be bound within the schemes they have created for themselves. The task of the analyst is, therefore, to understand the constitution of those schemes. The logical conclusion of this idea, taken to its extreme, is that it should be possible to classify everything an improviser plays. Indeed it is possible to find this kind of approach at play in a number of notable studies of jazz musicians. Thomas Owens's work on Charlie Parker famously catalogued a series of motifs that Parker employed again and again.[23] Lawrence Gushee demonstrated something similar with Lester Young, and Gregory Smith applied this idea to the work of Bill Evans.[24] But Corbett has something else in mind, something that helps to differentiate improvised music from other forms. Improvisers, he says, seek to play not what they know but what they do not know. Corbett poses the original question and provides another answer: "Old Pat Question: How does an improviser improvise? New Pat Answer: By developing and employing a repertoire of possibilities in order to risk the unknown."[25]

Corbett's position strikes a balance by accepting that improvisers function through using a set of practices and procedures that have been learned and internalized, while also creating a theoretical space for non-conformity, the potential for improvised music to escape the confines and consequences of this patterning. This lends an intriguing duality to improvisation, which Corbett describes as "the permanent play of threshold and transgression."[26] So it is that any approach to improvised music has to make a point of accommodating this dual approach: looking for conformity to patterns, but also moments where those patterns may be intentionally transgressed. Seen this way, another factor comes into play in understanding how we listen to improvised music: time, or temporality.

In a 2004 essay, pianist and theorist Vijay Iyer addresses the issue of temporality. Iyer begins by suggesting, following Alfred Schutz, that listening to music involves a sense of shared time that reading a book, for example, does not.[27] This temporal empathy between listener and performer becomes especially important in improvised music Iyer suggests, because:

> The experience of listening to music that is understood to be improvised differs significantly from listening knowingly to composed music. The main source of drama in improvised music is the sheer fact of the shared sense of time: the sense that the improviser is working, creating, generating musical material, in the same time in which we are co-performing as listeners.... In improvisational music, this embodied empathy extends to an awareness of the performers' coincident physical and mental exertion, of their "in-the-moment" (i.e., in-time) *process* of creative activity and interactivity.[28]

Improvisation has often been studied through modes of analysis that lay bare the music in much the same way as if it if were notes on the page. But Iyer identifies the potential for understanding it in terms of the act of listening, and how listeners hear the music in a temporality they share with the improviser. So it is that Corbett's aesthetic of risk is significant, because music can create the impression that the improviser is taking risks. This kind of effect has even guided the work of some scholars on Jarrett's improvisations. Take, for instance, Randall Bauer's classification of passages in Jarrett solo concerts. Bauer sets up a kind of binary between repetitive vamp passages and unstable "probing" passages: "There is much localized repetition in Jarrett's work, and very often he will choose something small and self-contained and stick with it for considerable time.... Occasionally one hears Jarrett probing for new material. He is trying to move from one large section to another, but needs to find his way to this new material, and often this process sounds very ruminative."[29] Bauer's classification of a probing section is based on hearing and equating a kind of musical exploration, characterized by the move through a range of harmonic areas and ideas, with a certain intention on Jarrett's part. A vamp passage comes to signify a fixation, as Bauer describes it, focusing on a particular harmony, groove, and piano figuration. A probing passage on the other hand represents the fact that the music is unsettled, and that the improviser is attempting to move it in a new direction. I argue it is not possible to assert that any particular passage tells us what the improviser is thinking. Rather, the music *affords* the possibility of being heard in this way. Harmonic or rhythmic simplicity can be heard as fixation, tedium, or joyousness, while instability can be heard as exploration, restlessness, probing, and so on. Because we hear the music in this moment-to-moment way, we experience what seems like empathy with the improviser. And because this is improvised music, even though we can replay a record countless times it seems to act as a window onto a creative moment. Not only is it possible to listen in this way, but the music creates this sense for us as we listen. In other words, the music encourages us to hear it as improvised and allows us to participate in the creation of a narrative about improvisation.

This then brings me back to the classification of musical types that I discussed earlier. This analytical approach is founded not on creating a taxonomy but on understanding the expressive function of musical types. In hearing this music as improvised, musical types afford particular interpretations. As Bauer suggests, a vamp passage seems to express a certain manner of fixation with rhythmic and harmonic material. A groove might seem harmonically tedious, but understood as part of a larger stylistic nexus it expresses a physical engagement and creates a stability based on the expectations that the music creates through repetition. A ballad passage, on the other hand, is much more open interpretively, because of the avoidance of cyclical sequences and steady meter/tempo. It can be said to convey a sense of exploration in the sense Bauer suggests. Taken together, these two styles also suggest more generally that ideas of expectations can come to be important factors in how we listen to improvised music.

This returns me to a question I raised at the start of this book, namely how Jarrett's records, *The Köln Concert* in particular, work as records of live performance. Rather than merely appearing to be live by virtue of their packaging and the sound of the audience on the recording, they create the sense of liveness. Perhaps it is the case that a quality of liveness emerges from the recording as a result of how listeners are inclined to share in this temporality with the improviser, to hear the music as it is being created and to understand it as such. It is not just that the music is improvised but that it *sounds* improvised. And it is with this in mind that I want to proceed next to dealing with the music of the recording itself, in order to try to understand how it creates this expressive effect.

CHAPTER 5

AT THIS POINT I turn to a discussion of the music of *The Köln Concert*. For quite understandable reasons, many scholars writing on jazz and popular music have come to be wary of music analysis. In part this is because of a perception that analysis deals in highly specialized concepts that have little to do with actually explaining how music works for listeners.[1] Although I acknowledge that analysis can sometimes be guilty of such a charge, there are very good reasons for using it as a tool. The dictum that jazz has developed as an oral tradition sometimes disguises the fact that musicians have always engaged with a range of theoretical ideas, no matter the nature of the language employed to describe such concepts. Harmonic knowledge is seen as part of what it means to be a competent jazz musician, as described by ethnomusicologist Paul Berliner in terms of how musicians acquire the knowledge to identify, and deal with, harmonic structures.[2] The very same thing can be observed from systems of jazz pedagogy, through educational texts or courses offered at institutions across the world. Both these things indicate the degree to which a practical grasp of theory is part of a jazz culture that, at the same time, also prizes innovation and artistry. From this perspective, to analyze the music of the Cologne concert is to interrogate it as part of a musical culture in which theoretical concepts are important and have a meaning to those who invest in that culture.

Listeners to the Cologne concert recording, both during the 1970s and subsequently, would likely have been aware of the idea of Jarrett as an improviser. But nothing on the artwork of the recording actually explains that the music is improvised. Underneath the track listing appears the text "All Composed by Keith Jarrett," which may even confuse matters for some listeners. Nonetheless Jarrett was well known as an improvising musician, and the music plays its part here by supporting that idea and reinforcing it to the listener. Even though the record is a material artifact that allows us to listen to a performance again and again, the fact that we are hearing an improvisation imbues the recording with an immediacy that works against the banality of repetition. Listening to improvised music affords the potential for a kind of engagement with the music if the listener is willing to invest in a set of cultural suppositions about improvisation. So this analysis engages with the Cologne recording as a piece of improvised music, by exploring some ideas about the kind of listening experience it affords.

A word on the music examples is also in order here. In 1991, Jarrett published an authorized transcription of *The Köln Concert*, completed by Yukiko Kishinami and Kuniko Yamashita.[3] Naturally, this transcription has made the analysis I undertake in this chapter all the easier, removing the need for me to transcribe the music. The reader is encouraged wherever possible to use the transcription while reading this section, although hopefully it will still suffice when read as is. All the music examples herein are drawn from the published transcription. Transcription is a highly subjective practice, in which one is forced to make choices at almost every turn. These choices often involve decisions about whether to aim for the utmost accuracy (which almost inevitably results in a considerable degree of notational complexity, especially in rhythmic terms) or to privilege clarity and readability. Pitch information can usually be represented accurately without too much difficulty, but rhythmic information is harder to process, especially in passages characterized by rubato or expressive manipulation of meter. And what often sounds like a very simple rhythm may require complex representation if accuracy is the primary goal, making it invariably look more complex than it sounds. So it is that most transcribers faced with this problem—and I believe this is true of *The Köln Concert* transcription—opt for the neater-looking solution. Information about articulation is usually placed further down the chain of importance from pitch and rhythm, mainly because of the view that transcription is a representation of a recorded performance, not an autonomous text.

But there are also sounds on the recording that are of great importance, for which there are no easy notational solutions. There are environmental sounds from the concert hall, audience noises, and the sounds Jarrett creates with the pedal for deliberately percussive effect. And there is Jarrett's vocalizing, an aspect of his playing that has proved controversial in the past, at least for some critics and listeners. Musicologist Jairo Moreno has argued that criticisms of Jarrett's vocalizing serve to reinforce a pervasive idea that music should be heard as autonomous from the necessary physicality that demands its creation.[4] Similarly Susan McClary writes in an essay on multimedia performer Laurie Anderson that Western culture has tended to "mask the fact that actual people usually produce the sounds that constitute music."[5] The sound of Jarrett vocalizing represents a physical trace of the performer on the sound recording, which serves as reminder of the kind of physicality I touched on in Chapter Two. Steven Termini posits a means of analyzing how Jarrett's vocalizations work in reference to the music, suggesting that "probably the most compelling aspect of Jarrett's vocalizations is what they suggest to us about intentions that are normally hidden from view, or, rather, from hearing."[6] Termini views the vocalizations as allowing the potential to hear when Jarrett is inspired or frustrated, or indeed finds something amusing. I would rather state that the vocalizations *afford* us the possibility of making these interpretations. What interests me is not so much whether such interpretations are correct, but the fact that the music prompts us to make them, to create a meaning out of these sounds.

"KÖLN PART I"

The Köln Concert opens with a simple five-note phrase. Quite recently, a story has appeared suggesting that this phrase did not simply appear from nowhere. The story has it that Jarrett was imitating the pre-concert bell at the Cologne Opera House, and that the audience can be heard laughing.[7] Indeed on careful listening it is possible to hear some laughter as soon as Jarrett starts. The music of this opening is significant for where it comes from and because it establishes some features that characterize not only the first few minutes of the improvisation but the whole recording. As we can see from the opening bars shown in Example 5.1, the

EXAMPLE 5.1   Opening of Köln, Part I

harmony of this opening is characterized by diatonic chords that either omit the third, or add ninths or fourths. The first harmony is a D chord with a suspended fourth (avoiding establishing major or minor sonority) followed by an A minor chord with added ninth, seventh (in passing), and fourth. In this opening passage there is no dominant seventh harmony at all, and none of the chromatic alterations that characterize post-bop jazz harmony: flattened fifths and ninths, sharpened fifths and ninths, and so on. All of this gives the music a very distinctive open diatonic sound, but in functional terms this is not a standard tonal system.

It is worth bearing in mind how harmony of this kind came to be established in jazz. Developments in jazz harmony since the 1940s are often thought to be following a path of development characterized by increasing complexity, with the atonality of free jazz as an extreme result. But this avoids seeing that simplification or reduction in harmonic terms is just as significant as increasing complexity, as for instance in the development of modal playing when the underlying harmonic structures of pieces became simpler but allowed musicians (notably John Coltrane) the freedom to superimpose increasingly complex material above. When at the end of the 1960s jazz musicians began to look to various forms of popular music as vehicles for performance, whether it was the Beatles or Bob Dylan, they encountered straightforward diatonic harmony. The nature of this harmony was such that it could not easily bear the kinds of harmonic alterations jazz musicians would typically have used with Broadway songs. The reason in part was because this new music was often composed on guitar and lacked the typical kinds of harmonic building blocks found in the jazz language. This approach to new material among jazz musicians was combined with a distinctive turn toward what jazz scholar David Ake calls the "Rural American Ideal."[8] Ake's discussion of Bill Frisell, Jarrett, and Pat Metheny identifies an invocation of a modern kind of pastoral mode, constructed through various signifiers such as timbre, cover art, song titles, and unaltered diatonic harmony.

Such a harmonic approach is particularly important to Jarrett in the Cologne performance. Other performances from the 1975 tour are not quite so reliant on this kind of harmony, and the Cologne performance seems to emphasize this aspect of Jarrett's language particularly strongly. Not only is the formation of the individual harmonies of interest here, but so is the way they function to create progressions. In Example 5.2 we can see the harmonies of the opening condensed into block chords. What is clear immediately is that even though these are diatonic harmonies, they do not function within a conventional tonal system. Consider D as the key center, for instance: the A chord would normally be a dominant seventh and not a minor harmony as here, and the F chord would be $^\flat$III, not the conventional III ($F^\#$ minor). If we take G as the key center, then things look rather more straightforward. The F chord can be interpreted as $^\flat$VII, implying a Mixolydian tonality. That kind of tonality was far from unusual for harmony of the time, and indeed the Beatles had made quite a virtue of using this particular sound, as Walter Everett demonstrates.[9]

These differing interpretations of key center may seem beside the point, because they disguise what is really important about the way the harmony works in this passage. Each harmony seems connected to the next, and the voice leading employed helps to reinforce that connection. But this is a very different kind of functional harmonic movement from what we might expect in a Tin Pan Alley song or jazz standard. That is not only because of the construction of the chords, but because what links them is not a sense of goal-directed progression but rather

EXAMPLE 5.2   Opening of Köln, Part I, Harmonic Reduction

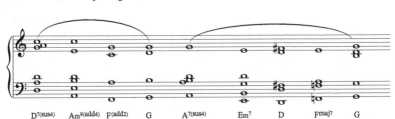

$D^{7(sus4)}$ $Am^{9(add4)}$ $F^{(add2)}$ G $A^{7(sus4)}$ Em^7 D F^{maj7} G

EXAMPLE 5.3   Opening of Köln, Part I, Phrase Structure

their membership of a harmonic system defined by the G key center. In this passage Jarrett creates a harmonic area by linking together a number of sonorities connected within this diatonic frame. The music unfolds without cadential points, and the harmonic sequence never follows the same path twice. As an improviser, Jarrett does not set out to create a harmonic sequence that he can cycle around, but instead he defines an area by iterating a number of chords among which he can move. This gives the music a sense both of foundation and of motion without establishing an ostinato or cyclical progression.

Other facets of this opening passage are worth elaborating on. The opening melodic statement undergoes a motivic development, so that its contour expands, providing a template underneath which the harmony and figuration can open out. As shown in Example 5.3, the first statement comprises four discrete phrases: in each case a short phrase followed by a longer answer. The second statement continues with four phrases, each modeled on the contour of the first set. This is not a highly organized melodic development, but it makes sense in the context of improvised music. Given the constraints of having to extemporize with a melodic phrase that has only just been played, it is perhaps to be expected that the result is not a perfectly shaped set of variations.

The harmony of this opening is, as we have seen, clearly defined within a harmonic area, yet without establishing an unequivocal key center. In rhythmic terms there is a gradual change that manifests itself slowly. The opening of the improvisation begins in a steady tempo but with music that is not heavily accentuated. Though the tempo is steady, this could not be said to be groove-based. But as the passage continues there is a move toward stronger rhythmic accentuation, taking the form of figures in the left hand that emphasize open fifths and create a kind of boogie-woogie inflection, as at 1'20".

At 1'50" in to the first part, Jarrett begins moving away from the harmonic axis of the opening. He does this through a strategy that he uses

EXAMPLE 5.4   2'12", B Locrian Vamp

in numerous contexts, employing a circle of fifths progression to move rapidly through a series of harmonies before landing in a new area. The progression here runs as a sequence of major harmonies: G–C–F–B♭–C–A–D–B–E–C♯m–F♯. The music then lands on a passage beginning at 2'12" (Example 5.4) formed from a vamp that is best described modally as B Locrian.

This passage feels important when it arrives because it sets up a series of expressive contrasts with what has gone before. The use of this distinctive-sounding minor mode with its flattened ninth degree (C) and dark-hued sound stands out in relation to the open diatonic sound of the opening. The harmonic stasis and repetitive figuration also marks out a different rate of change, implying a more static kind of music. And yet this new vamp does not last long: after all of thirty-nine seconds Jarrett brings the music out into a rubato passage on A minor at 2'52". The reason I draw attention to this short vamp passage is because it is marked out through difference. These musical contrasts suggest that it is a significant point in the improvisation because it marks a new direction. And yet, rather than this passage developing into an established groove, instead it gives way to something else after little more than half a minute.

What I am edging toward in describing the music this way is the sense that it affords us the possibility of hearing the mental exertions of the improviser. Heard this way what might seem like an inconsequential passage can actually become something quite interesting. We might consider that the vamp is a false start; it suggests Jarrett trying to move the music in a new direction (via the circle of fifths modulation), but unhappy with the idea that emerges, deciding instead to try a different strategy. Or we could see it as a deliberate attempt to play with expectations, alluding to the possibility of establishing a vamp, while not actually establishing it. As I have already suggested, these kinds of readings are always prone to failure in the sense that they are speculative. But this should not mean disregarding them entirely, because analyzing improvised music should involve engaging with the expressive effects music creates through the act of listening.

The rubato passage beginning at 2'52" is part of a much larger musical arch which takes over ten minutes to complete its trajectory. Although as I mentioned previously Gernot Blume segments this arch into a series of groove and rubato passages, his classification does not explore how these several types are connected.[10] The passage beginning at this point sets up a clear pattern whereby the left hand outlines the harmony through sounding individual chord tones in broken chord figuration, as seen in Example 5.5. Sometimes this harmony is sketched by the left hand in the barest terms, with simply a root and fifth. Because of the rubato feel, this broken-chord figuration does not have the sense it might normally of generating or articulating a pulse. At this point the harmony begins cycling around three chords: A minor, G major, and E minor. As the passage continues, Jarrett discards the E minor harmony and alternates between G major and A minor.

Over these bare left-hand harmonies the right hand plays what is, at the outset, a highly ornamented melodic improvisation confined to a small pitch space, which gradually opens out to long, sweeping right-hand lines. This whole passage is much less motivic in nature than the opening and is perhaps more aptly described as rhapsodic. For most of the time, the right hand lines do not use any chromatic tones from outside the A Aeolian mode (or the white keys of the piano). There are a couple of exceptions early on in the passage, including a particularly florid run where an $E^{7\#9}$ chord is substituted for the E minor. On the G chord Jarrett tends to avoid the seventh, which would define the chord either as a dominant or major seventh. The emphasis is, instead, largely pentatonic, with the collection G-A-B-D-E (G major pentatonic) particularly prominent.

The line shown in Example 5.5 extends over a G major/E minor sonority. The contour of this line here traces a large arc, from D_4 up to the B_5 at the end of the first bar, descending to B_3 two octaves below. Two patterns contained within this line are notable, the first being the initial upward/

EXAMPLE 5.5   Excerpt from Rhapsodic Passage

downward scalic sweep. The second is the descent, made up of a series of sequential downward scalic sweeps. Seen in notational form on the page, the sonic effect of these gestures does not come across adequately. There is a considerable amount of reverberation added to the recording. Though a certain amount comes from the hall itself, given that by Martin Wieland's account only two microphones were used to record the piano, relatively little of the hall's acoustic would have been captured; most of the reverberation would have been added in the studio. The result is that these scalic sweeps leave a subtle shimmering effect, so that rather than simply sounding like a series of rapidly executed notes there is an almost harp like quality about them. The sweeping nature of the line means that it serves a harmonic function, filling out the harmony implied by the bare left-hand part. That harmony is, as at the opening, enriched by the added ninths, sixths, and fourths that these sweeping lines include. These kinds of single-note lines are not typical of postbop jazz, in which the arpeggio is most often the device used to construct rapid motion. Instead of outlining harmony in a vertical sense as an arpeggio does by spelling out the chord, these patterns perform the same function in a linear sense, the difference being that they outline harmony through scalic means.

This passage also manifests an intensity that comes across on the recording as a sense of the ecstatic. But what is it that makes a device that appears musically simple so expressive? During this passage Jarrett can be heard singing along with some of these right-hand lines. Using Stephen Termini's categorization, these vocalizations are sometimes parallel to, and in tune with, the musical line, while at other times they are parallel but out of tune.[11] Vocalizing along with lines like this has an important effect: not only does it help convey for the listener the physical effort involved in improvising, but it also makes an implicit association with singing. From the point of view of technique, creating a long right-hand line simply involves the movement of fingers on keys, and it is not subject to the same physiological limitations as when a musician plays a wind instrument or sings. Singing along helps us hear the creation of these lines as an embodied act of performance that involves not just fingers on keys but the idea that those fingers are part of a performing body. At the same time as we hear singing in this passage, the right-hand lines are clearly beyond the capability of being sung in terms of their length, range, and rapidity. So these sung, but unsingable, lines are highly expressive, imbued with the physical agency of the voice and also ecstatic in the sense that they are impossible.

Toward the end of this passage at around 6'24" Jarrett adds some deliberate pedal noise, probably thumping his foot against the pedal while

EXAMPLE 5.6   New Figuration at 7'14"

not actually depressing it. The percussive effect resonates through the piano, and it articulates a slow four to a bar. This long rhapsodic episode then leads straight into the next phase at 7'14". Here the same harmonic sequence continues at the same tempo, but with a new figuration, as shown in Example 5.6.

The continuity with the previous section is important in terms of harmony and tempo, signaling that this is not a sudden change of direction. At this point we have moved from rubato to a steady tempo, and over the course of the next minute Jarrett continues with the G major/A minor ostinato shown in Example 5.6. But it rapidly turns from the minimal sounding pattern into something much grander. The articulation of the harmony on the first beat of every bar becomes heavily emphasized, with rolling left-hand octaves amplifying each shift. As Jarrett moves to a tremolo in his right hand toward the end of the passage (8'20"), so can be heard a number of his typical vocal expressions. Following Termini's categorization, these are what we might call "reactionary vocalizations." These sounds seem to signify reaction, or as Termini puts it, when Jarrett is "particularly pleased with the way an improvisation is transpiring."[12] The "whoos" Jarrett can be heard uttering at this point certainly serve, allied to the bombastic piano style of this particular passage, as an expression of joy.

All the considerable energy this passage creates is suddenly released as Jarrett lands on an A minor chord, and we return to the A minor/G major rubato/rhapsodic music at 8'39". Although the figuration is much as it was previously, now the music is inflected by many more chromatic pitches in the right hand than before, along with the occasional inclusion of D and E minor harmonies. Whereas before the A minor and G harmonies were largely uninflected, left open and clean, now the G chord is given the major seventh (F#) and the A minor its counterpart (G#). Example 5.7 shows an instance of this inflection of the diatonic harmony with these chromaticisms, specifically the raised seventh and flattened ninth over the A minor harmony. Overall this rhapsodic phase is shorter than its earlier counterpart, and after a short time it emerges in much the

EXAMPLE 5.7   Right Hand Lines with Chromatic Inflections

same way as before into a passage based on the same harmony, but with a fuller piano figuration (9'44"). This time the rhythmic sense is slightly different. There is no sustain pedal used here, so the playing is rhythmically emphasized, while the left hand creates a more complex pattern, resulting in a feel where the second sixteenth note of each beat is emphasized, as seen in Example 5.8.

As before, the harmonic connection with the previous music, and indeed the fact that Jarrett starts with the same melodic motif as that which closed the passage at 7'14", signals that this music is part of a larger structural whole. The following four minutes or so build on this groove, but there are some particular musical devices occurring during this passage that serve to create a sense of progression. At the start of the first phase (9'44" to 11'56"), the groove outlines the A minor to G ostinato. There is, from the outset, an implied D major inserted to facilitate the move from A minor to G major, as seen in Example 5.9. Over the course of this first phase the harmony becomes more and more pronounced,

EXAMPLE 5.8   Fuller Piano Figuration, 9'44"

EXAMPLE 5.9   Harmonic Sequence from Start and End of Phase

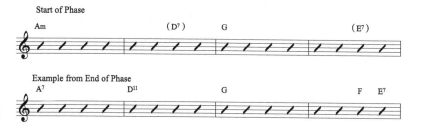

and is joined by other chords that have the effect of embellishing the sequence. Example 5.9 shows the chord sequence both at the start of the phase, and toward the end, when it is considerably embellished. The transformation of the A minor harmony to become a dominant seventh is significant, because it imbues the passage with a distinct blues inflection, supported by the use of the descending sequence from G to E[7] (V of A). But this is not strictly speaking a blues progression. It is instead the kind of passage that critics often label gospel-based, because of the use of dominant sevenths within a chordal ostinato supported by strong rhythmic left-hand figuration.

Alongside this developing harmonic sequence, there is a melodic strategy being worked out. The melodic phrase presented at the start of this section outlines a simple shape, with a rising sixth from E_4 to C_5 over the A minor chord, followed by a semiquaver descent to a B_4 over the G chord. This idea becomes the basis for a series of subsequent phrases that preserve its underlying shape, while adding considerable embellishments, much like the phrase structure at the very opening of the improvisation. After a little time the right-hand lines break free of this phrase structure altogether, and the effect is quite like the earlier rhapsodic music, with long, elaborate lines over the continuing groove maintained by the left hand.

This passage can be described via a familiar kind of formal archetype. The opening material is primarily melodic, its thematic status created through repetition. The virtuosic right-hand lines later on are something rather different, certain not thematically marked, more about ornamentation and display than thematicism. This overall pattern is of thematic material giving way to complex rhapsodic material, a progression that parallels one of the stereotypical formal features of jazz, namely the move from a composed thematic section to a complex improvised section, or from "head" to "solo." And this is a strategy that occurs again and again in the solo concerts; the exposition of material permits longer passages to be created using the same kinds of processes as a jazz musician might use when playing a standard tune. So the pattern employed in postbop jazz of head to solo still finds a manifestation in this context via this thematic-rhapsodic progression.

The second phase of this passage (11'56") moves toward a chordal approach with less in the way of elaborate right-hand lines, while effecting a highly distinctive harmonic change by replacing the A minor chord with a dominant. At this point Jarrett's left hand makes use of the bass registers of the piano, articulating rhythmically charged root notes with short arpeggiated figures. This reinforcement of the harmony in the left hand serves to strengthen the gospel inflection. In the third phase, at 12'51", the music returns to A minor and to something closer to the figuration heard at the start of the passage. At this point there is the first real clue that the music may be about to move somewhere new, with a particular harmonic hint that might take us beyond the A minor/G major axis. This comes at 12'59" when Jarrett moves to a Bb chord before moving back via a ii-V-I progression in A minor. This may be merely a momentary inflection but it is significant in the context, as it defies the expectations created by repetition within the passage. While the music proceeds for a time as if nothing has happened, at 13'48" Jarrett departs from A minor/G via the familiar circle of fifths device, moving through E^b to C, F, B^b, E^b, and so on. At this point the groove gradually dissipates as the music moves back toward an unsteady rubato.

Seen in the context of this passage, these two musical signals are unmistakable. The harmonic shift from A minor/G through what is an unstable progression (in that it takes us through a whole series of potential key centers), and the shift in rhythmic gear from groove back to rubato, has a highly dramatic effect. I have described elsewhere a similar example from the 1973 Lausanne concert, recorded on the *Solo Concerts* album.[13] In that case Jarrett seems intentionally to derail the momentum of the whole passage by introducing a rhythmically disruptive device, as if to force the music out of its set direction. And while this interruption is not as dramatic, it is clear that certain musical devices are used in order to force a way out of the set harmonic/rhythmic direction.

THOUGHTS ON OPENINGS

If I listen to the Köln concert, I hear all the things I would have shortened, you know, like why did I keep on playing all those meaningless improvi-

sations on top of that little G major thing that I started so beautifully
with?…After a certain time, after a certain amount of playing I knew
that was too much. But I didn't know that back when I did it.[14]

I will consider the overall shape of the first Cologne improvisation a little
later, but for now it is worth reflecting on the music I have discussed this
far. Jarrett's remarks to writer and broadcaster Alyn Shipton quoted here
reveal a rather interesting view of the first part of the concert. As the
preceding discussion has shown, there is quite an amount of music from
the first fifteen minutes based on a G major/A minor sequence. In fact,
other than one interruption with the short vamp at 2'12", the G major/
A minor axis remains unchallenged. It is only in the final passage that
the harmony opens out into a richer chord sequence, a moment that
proves to be the apex of this musical arch. But why should Jarrett label
this music as "meaningless" and conclude that he simply did not know at
the time when it was too much?

The span of this passage is marked out by a series of alternations between rubato and groove passages. But, regardless of these changes of
feel, the harmonic foundation remains the same. This creates some interesting expressive effects that do not occur in Jarrett's other recorded solo
concerts, at least up until Cologne. Because the harmonic underpinning
of this music remains unchanged, the result is that other kinds of musical shifts take on increased importance. The effect of moving from one
phase to another implies a sense of change and forward motion, but the
harmony implies a certain kind of stasis.

Is it possible to suggest that the particular kind of structure employed
in the Cologne performance has an expressive effect that other Jarrett
solo recordings do not? It is certainly true that compared to many of the
other recorded performances from around the time, both released and
unreleased, this opening is prone to uncharacteristically static harmony.
Jarrett generally seems to have liked to begin a solo concert with a ballad,
a style that fostered harmonic exploration. As we saw in Chapter Four, a
number of the improvisations from the 1975 tour begin with a minor-key
vamp with quartal harmony. Although it is difficult to generalize, the fact
that the Cologne performance opens with nearly fifteen minutes of music
based on an unchanging harmonic premise, and that there is a preva-
lence of unaltered diatonic harmony, does seem to mark this performance out from many of the others Jarrett gave around the same time.

But what of Jarrett's view that this whole passage was simply "too much,"
and that part of the improvisation was "meaningless," perhaps because it
did not progress harmonically? Certainly the recorded solo concert

improvisations from around this time evidence a concern with harmonic exploration tempered with static groove passages. This points to a tension between what Jarrett seems to have wanted to articulate in writings such as the liner notes to the 1973 *Solo Concerts* album and his views as expressed more recently, as in this 2005 interview with Shipton. The *Solo Concerts* liner notes articulate the idea of a shared responsibility between artist and audience, suggesting that Jarrett is not the creator but a channel for the creative.[15] Yet by suggesting that he did not know when it was "enough," his own subjectivity reveals itself, in the idea that the music was shaped by his (relative) youth and inexperience. His ambivalence in recent times toward the recording reveals the degree to which public perception clashes with his own views on its limitations. All this points to the importance of looking at how the recording can afford such different readings, placed in the context of the adulation it has received from many listeners, but also the disappointment Jarrett seems to feel over its shortcomings. As we will see in Chapter Seven, Jarrett's ambivalence may relate not only to the music of the performance but the way the record has come to be appropriated for ends other than those for which it was intended.

PART I, 14′14″

The passage beginning at around 14′14″ and continuing until 21′20″ marks a sharp contrast with the first fourteen minutes of music, being more harmonically mobile than previously. It moves through a range of key areas, and although it seems to foreground certain keys at various points, it is not until the emergence of A major at around 21″00′ that one clear tonality is established. It is worth approaching this passage by establishing how it differs musically from the opening fourteen minutes. There are no ostinatos or groove sections here, and no repeated sequences. By and large the music is permeated by a kind of rubato, and indeed the published transcription includes various annotations such as "tempo rubato," "slower rubato," and "flowing," all shorthand for a variety of rhythmic feels. The fact that this passage lacks these markers of harmonic and rhythmic stability creates a sense of detachment with what has gone before. It is tempting, when confronted by parts of Jarrett's improvisations that are so mobile, to think of the music as rambling, lacking any sense of stability, detached from idea, theme, and direction. But it is far more productive to consider how these sensations are created musically, and in the case of this passage there are musical devices that give us some idea of what kinds of organizational strategies might be at work. To begin, I am going to suggest a rough segmentation of this passage into phases, as

TABLE 5.1   Phases from Köln, Part I, 14'14" onwards

14'14"   Ballad, beginning in E^b major

15'06"   Choralelike passage in C major, becoming more expansive before
          ascending to:

16'36"   High-register chords, C minor with altered diatonic harmonies

17'45"   Melodic statements in octaves, punctuated by lower-register chords

18'45"   Expansive textures with left-hand octave bass notes

19'48"   Quieter melodic idea over a simple chordal accompaniment, leading to:

20'06"   Repeated A major chord, gradually leading into groove passage

shown in Table 5.1. Segmented this way, the passage reveals a dramatic trajectory, moving from a harmonically restless ballad into a chorale like episode, ascending to the upper registers, opening out into a declamatory passage beginning at 17'45", before gradually subsiding.

I have already mentioned Jarrett's use of a kind of simple-complex paradigm, or thematic-rhapsodic model, resembling the kind of head-solo template often used by jazz musicians. A melodic idea can be stated and gradually embellished through improvisation until it becomes something completely different, without any relation to the original, save the harmonic context in which it is used. The opening fourteen minutes of the Cologne concert contain much music that emulates the effect of improvised lines in jazz, specifically rapid melodic motion over a clearly articulated harmonic backdrop. This passage is very different, in the sense that it is highly motivic throughout and lacks the same thematic-to-rhapsodic progression. In this light it is interesting to consider how the melodic material is constructed, whether it simply works on a moment-to-moment basis, or if there are examples of any kind of developmental or variation processes.

Example 5.10 presents a series of melodic extracts taken from this passage. At the outset the melodic idea in question is characterized by a rising fourth with a stepwise descent to a tone below its starting point, before returning to the starting pitch. This idea then appears with slightly different rhythmic treatment at two transpositions (15'31" and 15"41). The idea at 16'54" is slightly different again, but based on the same contour, using a rising fourth with stepwise descent. The following few iterations are all in C minor, save for one brief conversion to the major at 18'21", while from 18'45" the motive is presented in a series of keys. Example 5.10

EXAMPLE 5.10   Motivic Development

KEITH JARRETT'S *THE KÖLN CONCERT*

indicates just a little of how this idea is worked through several keys, with rhythmic and melodic alterations, and suggests that its function is to provide a cohesive force.

The entry on "Improvisation" in *Grove Music Online* outlines a set of techniques or procedures in jazz, described as "common or even standard": paraphrase improvisation (the variation of a theme), formulaic improvisation (the use of a set of diverse motives and ideas), and motivic improvisation (the development of a single motive). As the entry states with regard to motivic improvisation, "musical ideas in this type of improvisation call attention to themselves by the way in which they are treated, and indeed they must be recognized and followed through a piece or section if the music is to be properly appreciated."[16] It is clear that Jarrett's way of working with this motive in this passage is much akin to motivic improvisation. We can find a similar kind of approach in Jarrett's treatment of standards with his trio (Gary Peacock and Jack DeJohnette), as discussed by Philip Strange and Steven Termini. Strange identifies in a number of Jarrett trio performances what he calls a procedure of "evolving motives," whereby Jarrett will develop melodic phrases sometimes derived from the melody of the composition through a number of choruses of an improvisation.[17] Termini points out how, in the opening to Jarrett's recording of "Autumn Leaves" from *Keith Jarrett at the Blue Note* (1994), he plays a solo introduction using motifs drawn from the song itself, in a way he describes as a "motivic and organic development."[18]

The harmonic approach in this passage is also worthy of some attention. Termini suggests that certain passages in Jarrett's music can be considered through the idea of what he calls "spontaneous modal shifts":

> Even while the bass, melody, or inner lines move through various permutations, they nevertheless remain for some time exclusively within a particular mode, regardless of texture, counterpoint or chord voicings. It is as if all the notes of a particular mode have "lit up" on the piano, and Jarrett plays his diverse ideas using only those notes. Then all at once, a new set of notes "lights up" and Jarrett seamlessly continues the improvisation using the new set of notes (i.e., the new modal template).[19]

Termini's approach is to consider the modal derivation of passages, rather than identifying harmony by means of a series of vertical sonorities, as is usually the case in jazz. This is an interesting approach because, often, Jarrett's playing is highly diatonic in the moment-to-moment sense,

EXAMPLE 5.11   Modal Shifts

while the overall harmonic effect is far from conventional. Example 5.11 shows a passage from 15'13" with Termini's modal templates indicated.

Whether to consider harmony in terms of modal area or diatonic progression (sometimes seen as a horizontal versus a vertical approach) is often a complex question. Modality and diatonicism are, far from being polar opposites, better described as two sides of the same coin. But leaving that question aside, Termini's approach does suggest that key centers (as represented by these modal templates) are not expressed through conventional diatonic means (the occasional V-I cadence notwithstanding). Instead key centers, whether implied or explicitly established, function as scalic generators of harmony. In the case of this passage, the E^b mode turns out to be significant. And when Jarrett moves to other modal areas (A^b and D^b), they are closely related to the E^b area via the circle of fifths. This is not to say that this passage emphasizes E^b major as a tonic key, however, but rather that its underlying organization is dependent on the E^b major mode.

EXAMPLE 5.12   20'06"

Having established the manner in which this passage works within flat keys and related modal areas, the move to A major at 20'06" is highly dramatic. Jarrett has moved out of flat keys into an area based roughly around G; at this point he states the earlier motivic idea in A major, with an A chord decorated with added ninth (Example 5.12). While pausing on this chord, he then continues by arpeggiating the chords downward in harp like fashion with pedal held down, creating a rich sonority. As this repetition continues, so the chord thickens into a diatonic cluster, with the fourth added both at the top and in the tenor register.

This particular moment in the improvisation is highly dramatic, understood in context. As I have already suggested, Jarrett's improvisations generate particular kinds of expectations based on harmonic, rhythmic, and gestural norms. Music that is noticeably different from what has gone before will be marked, heard as significant by virtue of how we listen to these improvisations. The passage that went before established a harmonic mobility to the music, thus creating an expectation of further movement. But when the A major harmony emerges it marks an extreme harmonic, gestural, and rhythmic stasis. The iteration of these chords dominates the music, and the fragmentary notes that Jarrett adds in between each chord seem of little importance. This kind of sudden musical disparity, the move from a passage that is harmonically, rhythmically, and texturally active into music in which the whole point is inactivity, creates the sense of a dramatic intrusion, or interruption. The change is so marked that this seems like a rupture in the musical flow.

This moment can be understood by drawing on the argument I have already presented about listening to *The Köln Concert* as a piece of improvised music. Because we experience a sense of shared time with the improviser while listening, the music affords the opportunity of being heard as a reflection of the creative process. Moments such as this can be understood in terms of not only musical factors, but what such factors might serve to suggest. The sense is that this moment arrives suddenly, almost out of nowhere. Musically this is an unusually minimal gesture for Jarrett: a single chord, played again and again albeit with broadening emphasis, punctuated by pauses as the notes linger. Yet the A major tonality does not rupture the musical flow. Its significance becomes clear only as it is repeated, and it is the nature of this repetition that serves to make it more and more significant every time the chord is sounded. The sense is that something happens in the music that is beyond the improviser's control or intention. This sense of non intention is contributed to by Jarrett's seeming to stumble onto this A major chord, and then after hearing it, repeating it again and again. What seems like a fairly arbitrary musical idea, simply one of a series of chords in this passage, suddenly becomes something quite different and highly significant. Naturally, reading improvised music in this way introduces a degree of listener subjectivity into the equation. But the cultural baggage that Jarrett's solo concerts have acquired through a variety of means primes and encourages us to hear the music in this way.

The passage that leads out of this A major episode continues in the same tonality but with a groove figuration, and proceeds until the end of the improvisation. Although it retains A major throughout via a left-hand ostinato, the right hand implies an A-D-E progression, as shown in Example 5.13.

As earlier in the improvisation, what is striking here is the fact that this entire passage articulates an uninflected A major. The only exception is a short sequence at 23'20" where Jarrett moves downward from the A major harmony by step before reaching D major, then returning to the A vamp. The passage moves into a second phase at 23'56" with the introduction of demisemiquaver rhythms, as shown in Example 5.13. This

EXAMPLE 5.13   A Major Vamp

KEITH JARRETT'S *THE KÖLN CONCERT*

passage is, as with some of the earlier vamp episodes that break up the rhapsodic music, concerned more with articulating harmony and groove than providing a foundation over which Jarrett can solo. The vamp itself is far more than just a left-hand figure. There is the inner part in Jarrett's right hand, played around the tenor region of the piano, which works in combination with the rhythms of the left hand. This has the effect of constraining how far the right hand can move without dispensing with this aspect of the groove. At the point where the rhythms intensify, the vamp becomes more straightforwardly chordal, now just with iterations of D and A major harmonies through these rhythmically articulated chords. This pure rhythmic articulation of harmony is one of those moments in this music that look quite bland on the page but sound anything but on the recording. In large part, this is down to Jarrett's ability to create and maintain a groove, something I examine in more detail in the next chapter. There is a sense that, as this first part of the improvisation draws to its close, the move from melody to a pure rhythmically charged harmony functions as a kind of ending gesture. Indeed, the closing section of the first improvisation from the 1973 Lausanne concert (from the *Solo Concerts* LP) works in a very similar way.[20]

STRUCTURE AND EXPRESSION

Although the localized musical strategies I have identified in the first Cologne improvisation can be expressive, so the overall shape of the improvisation is significant. Table 5.2 presents one possible structural interpretation of the improvisation. One of the main assumptions here is that whereas a change of rhythmic feel, from rubato to groove and back, can prompt a sense of structural division, harmonic consistency can create a connection allowing two passages to be experienced as part of a larger structural whole.

In this improvisation there are a number of rhythmic feels; the steady feel of the opening, a number of groove sections including the closing passage, as well as rubato sections. The alternation of rubato and groove feels sets up an oscillation between music that is grounded and rhythmic, and music that is much more fluid. I have already described the manifestation of this effect with the music based on the A minor/G ostinato, but it is also articulated over a larger scale, as Table 5.2 demonstrates. Clearly the most unstable passage of the improvisation begins at the fourteen minute mark and contains music that is highly mobile harmonically and texturally, but it also returns us to a static groove passage that closes the improvisation. The equation of music that is rhythmic and

TABLE 5.2   Structure of Köln, Part I

Time	Part	Tonality	Description
0'00"	**Opening**	Am/G	Steady, opening melodic theme expands
2'12"	Vamp	B Locrian	Vamp figuration, nonthematic
2'52"	**Rhapsodic passage**		
	Phase 1, rhapsodic	Am/G (ostinato)	Rubato, bare left hand, long and elaborate right-hand lines
7'42"	Phase 2, groove	Am/G (ostinato)	Steady, simple descending theme
8'40"	Phase 3, rhapsodic	Am/G (ostinato)	Rubato, as before, more chromatic
9'44"	Phase 4, groove	Am/G, broadening to Am-G-F-E⁷	LH ostinato, then octaves
14'14"	**Ballad passage**	Begins in E♭, explores flat keys	Exploratory
15'06"	Choralelike		
16'35"	High-register chorale	C minor area	
17'45"	Melodic statements in octaves		
21'13"	**Groove passage**	A major (with D and E implied)	Vamp

harmonically grounded with stability, and that which is pulseless (or at least metrically ambiguous) and lacks a clearly established tonal or modal center with instability, suggests that these large-scale contrasts may prompt the construction of narratives about improvisation. One possible narrative archetype here is that of starting-exploration-return. The music begins in a way that seems fairly regular and ordered, through its invocation of a diatonic harmonic area coupled with a certain kind of phrase structure. The episodes that follow, where it opens out into more expansive texture, are always followed by returns, to music that is decidedly motivic, while the long central section represents a sustained push into foreign territory, only to return. That sense of large-scale musical progression from the stable to the unstable and back again could be read as a simple but effective metaphor for the act of improvisation, and one that encapsulates many of the ideas about the creative act Jarrett had been articulating.

One of the questions I posed at the end of Chapter Two regards how the music of *The Köln Concert* fits into the context of the readings some musicologists, Sheila Whiteley in particular, make of rock music of the late 1960s and 1970s. Such readings identify a number of musical factors—electronic alteration of sounds (either in the studio or through effects pedals), and use of extended forms (particularly in progressive rock)—that can be said to evoke an altered sense of time or state.[21] But there is a difficulty many find with readings like these. It is one thing to say that music might have the potential to be heard in this way, but quite another that it is actually coded with this meaning. For Tia DeNora, whose work I return to in Chapter Seven, some musicological approaches to the question of music's expressive force take a theoretical shortcut, which neglects to survey whether music actually does what is sometimes claimed for it. She suggests that it is necessary to investigate "how music is actually read and pressed into use by others, how music actually comes to work in specific situations and moments of appropriation."[22] In Chapter Seven I look a little further at the evidence for how *The Köln Concert* has come to be seen in this way. But it is worth considering what musical codes there are in the first improvisation that might prompt the kinds of readings Whiteley makes.

The most striking musical device is the use of long sections of music that do not shift harmonically. This harmonic stasis is expressed in two ways in the first improvisation, in one instance through a groove and in another through highly rhapsodic virtuosity. This in itself is nothing unusual for Jarrett, as almost all of his solo concert performances around this time seem to have contained such passages. The repetitive drone-based vamp passages he plays in these improvisations are often heard as tedious, signals of Jarrett toying with simple materials for want of a better idea. But it is also possible to hear these passages rather differently. Given their penchant for repetition over and above any conventional kind of musical discourse, they can be heard to articulate an alternative, decidedly non-Western kind of temporality. Neil Tesser, writing a review of the *Sun Bear Concerts* (1976) for *Down Beat*, commented on Jarrett's vamp passages: "these are not ostinatos around which Jarrett dances melodic ballet, nor are they his equivalent of simple mark-time riffing. They are sonic mandalas. The album notes include the advice 'Think of your ears as eyes,' and just as mandalas are often stared at to induce meditational trance, these patterns can be 'stared' at to produce transcendent results."[23]

Tesser's review serves to confirm that Jarrett's music was heard, by some listeners, in terms of a non-Western aesthetic. A certain kind of musical stasis, executed by means of harmonically immobile vamp passages, was part of a more general cultural potential music could possess to evoke altered states of consciousness. A wide range of other music from the decade was ascribed a similar power, most notably perhaps the minimalism of Steve Reich and Philip Glass, with its non-Western overtones emphasized by those composers' engagement with Indian and African musics. The harmonic stasis in parts of the Cologne improvisations does not necessarily have to be seen as meaningless in the sense Jarrett suggests, then, but potentially highly meaningful. Understood against the background of ideas contemporary to the 1970s regarding music's power to evoke ideas about experience and the self, such music can be seen to evoke a notion about the potential the act of listening held for listeners, a potential that is in itself part of the reception history of *The Köln Concert.*

CHAPTER 6

"KÖLN PART IIA"

The second part of the Cologne performance is divided into three parts on the recording: "Part IIa," "Part IIb," and "Part IIc." This is somewhat curious, because usually Jarrett's format in playing solo concerts during the early 1970s was to improvise two halves of music (usually each around the half-hour mark in length) with encores at the end.[1] On the 1973 *Solo Concerts* release the Bremen and Lausanne performances were divided over the sides of three LPs, giving the track order "Bremen Part I," "Part IIa," "Part IIb," "Lausanne Part Ia," "Part Ib," "Part IIa," "Part IIb." The track listing demarcated the two main improvisations for each concert, while also acknowledging the split created by the division across multiple LPs. However, on the CD release, while the Bremen performance became "Part I" and "Part II," both Lausanne improvisations were merged into a single sixty-four-minute track. This inconsistency also applies to *The Köln Concert*. The demarcation of the second improvisation into three segments would have suited the LP format, but on CD the track listing is retained. This means that "Part IIa" and "Part IIb" are still separate tracks, although taken together they make up one continuous improvisation. The tracks on the CD are created in such a way that one runs straight into the other; nonetheless, the demarcation still seems somewhat unusual. As I discuss later on, "Part IIc" is the encore to the performance and for a number of reasons has to be viewed differently from the rest of the recording.

The second improvisation from the Cologne concert opens with a lengthy (eight-minute) groove passage in D major. In many respects, this has many of the same characteristics as the groove passages from the first improvisation, in that it begins in an uninflected D major with the gradual appearance of chromatic alterations as it proceeds. It is worth considering this groove passage in rather more detail, not least because it serves as a good example of how Jarrett generally constructs passages such as this.

Groove is usually described in terms of two concepts, one being a specifically musical characteristic, the other an experiential quality.[2] The musical characteristic is a repeated figure, usually in the form of an ostinato. But it is obvious that not all music using a repeated figure can be said to employ a groove. The second quality, then, is important in defining a groove. Usually a groove is thought to create a particular kind of rhythmic characteristic that can be experienced physically. It has a sense, as ethnomusicologist Stephen Feld describes, of drawing in the listener.[3] Ingrid Monson points out how many jazz musicians think of groove in terms of a certain kind of feeling.[4] Along with this description of groove as musical device and expressive effect, there is a use of the term that occurs in the label "groove-based music." In a groove-based music such as funk, groove comes to act as a guiding principle, whereby multiple parts lock together to form composite textures. Good examples might be the work of James Brown, or the way grooves are constructed on Herbie Hancock's *Headhunters* album.[5] Jazz is not usually thought of as a groove-based music because even though there is significant emphasis on creating a rhythmic structure through the interaction of different parts, usually musicians exercise significant freedom in constructing their lines in a way that is not generally true of groove-based musics.

There is an important tradition within jazz of the piano acting as the generator of groove in a solo context. In styles such as boogie-woogie, stride, and ragtime, the left hand functions both to generate rhythmic momentum through a repeated figure as well as to articulate harmony. This dual role is inherently virtuosic, in that particularly with accomplished practitioners it demonstrates independence of the two hands.

Both seem to be doing completely different, but simultaneously related, things. The virtuosic effect comes from the juxtaposition of the two parts rather than the constitution of either one. There are times in Jarrett's improvisations where there are definite hints of boogie-woogie, namely in passages where the left hand maintains a simple vamp pattern with the right hand working melodically against it. But there are other passages, and the opening of the second part of the Cologne concert is a good example, where the two hands work together in quite another way. Rather than a clear demarcation between right and left hands, whereby one serves a melodic function and the other rhythmic/harmonic, in this case both hands work in much the same way. This interlocking is both literal and metaphoric. There is an effect whereby the rhythms in both hands create a resultant pattern when combined, in this case partly because of the limited two-octave span the passage starts in, meaning that distinguishing between the two hands by ear is almost impossible.

There is also a physical interlocking here suggested by the authorized transcription, and supported by existing video evidence. Footage exists of Jarrett performing solo in Perugia, Italy, in the summer of 1974.[6] During one particular section, he plays an A minor groove passage that sustains repeated As in eighth notes in the tenor voice. Even without close-ups, it is possible to discern from the footage that Jarrett manages this by alternating the thumbs of both hands on that particular key. Throughout the D groove passage in the transcription of *The Köln Concert*, there are indications that some of the notes on the lower stave are played by the thumb of the right hand. These annotations may have been made in part for the amateur musician wanting to emulate Jarrett's performance, but they also point to the possibility that when this passage was played he employed some of this interlocking to facilitate the left-hand motion.

The overall effect of this juxtaposition of hands is a groove that is polyphonic: there are multiple parts, lines, and voices, but they all function as a cohesive whole. This combination of layers makes passages like this very much akin to groove-based musics, in that the overall rhythmic sense results from a combination of lines melded together, rather than any single part. The opening two bars of this particular groove passage help establish the rhythmic sense of the opening, as shown in Example 6.1.

This opening has a somewhat irregular accentual pattern, at least compared with the passage as a whole. The initial downbeat is articulated by a D_2, played probably with the little finger of the left hand. Most likely the repeated Ds an octave above (D_3) are played by alternating thumb and index finger. But even though that first D_2 articulates the

EXAMPLE 6.1   Opening of Köln, Part IIa

downbeat, over the next few bars it fails to do likewise, and it is displaced on its appearance in the fourth bar. In the second and fourth bars of this passage there is no left-hand articulation of the downbeat at all. This is, in part, because the main emphasis in this passage is on the backbeat, that is the second and fourth beats of the 4/4 meter. In this case, the opening bars of the passage represent the establishment of the groove, and in order to understand the rhythmic basis on which it is built, it is rather better to look at an example some bars in.

In Example 6.2, we can see that the D_2 functions to articulate the downbeat as at the outset. But what notation singularly fails to do, in the case of a passage like this, is to establish the accentual pattern. If all of these pitches were played, as the notation suggests, largely uniformly, the result would be a series of unaccented notes in even time. In these kinds of passages the shortcomings of notation are exposed. Here there is an accentual pattern at work that creates a uniform rhythmic emphasis from bar to bar. It is not so much that certain notes are accented, or

EXAMPLE 6.2   Groove Passage with Accentual Pattern

simply played louder than others, but rather that they are emphasized by virtue of their articulation. The small staff above the piano parts in Example 6.2 shows this accentual pattern. Here it is the downbeat that is actually the weakest of the three pulses. The backbeat emphasis comes from the placement of accents on the second and fourth beats. In addition, there is a "pushed" third beat, placed on a sixteenth-note offbeat. We can see two ways in which this is articulated. In the first bar the right hand emphasizes this pushed beat by holding the syncopated chord over the third quarter-note beat, while the left hand continues with sixteenth notes. In the second bar, the left hand also holds over the beat, thus emphasizing this accent.

We can use this accentual framework as a means of defining the first phase of this groove passage. When the music reaches 1'38", the second phase of the passage begins in which Jarrett's right hand solos over the vamp, the left hand taking on the role of maintaining the groove. What is interesting here is a subtle shift in feel, away from the backbeat-related pattern, and closer to a straight four. In some ways this is inevitable because right hand and left diverge rather like soloist and rhythm section. The result is that the accentual pattern is pushed to the background. What helps create the sense of a "four" on the recording is not merely the notes sounded on the piano, but the sound of Jarrett's foot on the pedal. Pedal noise is a device he uses deliberately elsewhere. In this case the noise is not of a sufficient volume to be audible above the notes, but it functions in auditory terms almost like a bass drum, placed low in the mix, articulating the four beats of the meter. It is also placed slightly ahead of the beat, having the effect of propelling the music by anticipating the beat.

Of equal interest is the construction of Jarrett's left-hand vamp patterns at this point. Naturally we think of vamp patterns as being repeated ostinato figures, and in groove-based music this is always the case. But in Jarrett's vamp passages there is a subtle process of variation at work, whereby the details at the micro level change constantly, while the overall template of the vamp remains unchanged. The effect is that the vamp always sounds the same, and yet it is almost impossible to define by one invariant pattern. A quick glance at Jarrett's left hand from 2'13" explains this very well. The five-bar passage in Example 6.3 demonstrates how the left-hand pattern can differ in every bar.

This process of variation seen across five bars also takes place on a larger scale across the whole passage. What is clear from Example 6.3 is that, even though every bar is different, they are all derived from the same underlying template. There is a fairly simple explanation for a certain amount of this left-hand variation, which accounts for many of

EXAMPLE 6.3   D Major Vamp Variants, 2'13"

these localized differences. Most of the variation occurs rhythmically, in the playing of the D₃ on the middle of the bass stave. It is probable these notes would have been played by alternating the thumb and index finger of the left hand. There is a close connection between the density of pitches in the left hand and the activity in the right hand. Thus, when Jarrett's right hand executes a rapid solo flurry, often the activity in the left hand pares down and becomes momentarily rather simpler. Conversely, when there is a pause in right-hand activity, the density of pitches in the left hand often increases, as in the streams of sixteenth notes shown in the last bar of Example 6.3. In part this can be seen as a natural physical response: the coordination required to keep a regular and demanding left-hand pattern going with a florid right hand line simply means that the left hand will become sparser at moments when the right hand is particularly active.

At the same time as this localized variation, there are also larger shifts of level that occur during the passage and influence how the vamp is constructed. The first is a strategy I have already mentioned, which is the move from a purely diatonic harmony toward a blues-inflected one. Thus, the pure D major of the opening begins to be inflected from 2'24" with the dominant seventh C, and then in some of the right-hand runs that follow, the sharpened ninth, F, is used alongside the major third F#, in a typical blues manner. The second is the introduction of a new pitch into the vamp at 2'54". The use of the G in the bassline as a passing note onto the A creates a distinctive kind of rolling effect as the vamp now starts to imply a harmony additional to the D major. Both changes can be seen in Example 6.4.

There are two points within the passage where Jarrett inserts material that could be described as akin to a "breakdown" section. The first is relatively brief, coming at 4'34" where the rhythmic movement in the left hand suddenly switches to syncopated chords, creating a hemiola effect against the pulsating triads in the right hand. This is just a momentary effect, but it is significant for two reasons. First, this is a strategy Jarrett uses in other

EXAMPLE 6.4   Modifications to D Vamp

improvisations to effect a transition out of a groove section. There is a particularly interesting example from the 1973 Lausanne concert (from *Solo
Concerts*) that I have discussed elsewhere.[7] Second, it serves, for the first
time in the improvisation, to break out of the accentual pattern established
almost from the outset. And even though this is a momentary rhythmic
departure, it signals the possibility of breaking down the vamp at some
point. The second breakdown is much more substantial and certainly
worthy of the name. This occurs at 5'50", when the rhythmic momentum
stops altogether. Jarrett effects a sudden move to a B^{b7} chord where he
pauses before in typical fashion moving to E^{b7}, sidestepping to E^7 and then
A^7, where there is a stop-time break as a right-hand solo line in sixteenth
notes leads over the move back into the vamp. This device is one Jarrett
employs regularly in groove passages, permitting a brief departure from
the vamp via a circle-of-fifths-related sequence.

After these two instances, the third time Jarrett departs from the rhythmic template of the groove, it is for a passage that effects a transition to an
entirely new musical area. This begins at 7'09" and ends at 7'57". Over the
course of a minute, the left hand articulates a stepwise movement from F♯
to E to D in a variety of rhythmic patterns. The right hand outlines a hammered D major sonority, usually in the form of an open fifth chord, as
seen in Example 6.5. The use of the sustain pedal means that the previously clear and crisp texture becomes increasingly blurred.

EXAMPLE 6.5   Transition Passage, 7'09"

In notational terms, this passage presents a particularly vivid illustration of the limitations of transcription. In the preface to the published transcription of the improvisation, Jarrett writes, "on pages 50 and 51 of Part IIa there is no way to obtain on paper, the real rhythmic sense of this section. There is much more going on on the recording, but this 'going on' does not always translate into notes on paper."[8] The passage he is referring to is this transition. The manner of notation used in the transcription gives a very poor indication of the sonic effect at this point, not just due to the fact that no pedal marks are included. This is because there are instances where the sonic information on a recording is not sufficient to give absolute determination of the notes being played by the improviser. The kinds of tools currently available for transcribers permit recordings to be slowed down without any alteration of pitch, something particularly useful in the case of passages such as this. But slowing this passage down serves only to reveal the problem in more detail. The attacks in the right hand are particularly strong, and the use of the sustain pedal means that, for much of the time, only the sustains of the left-hand pitches can be heard. Attacks are almost completely masked in places by the hammered right-hand chords. The process of transcription here has been hampered by the sonic complexity of the recording. Usually this is the case with recordings made on poor equipment, where the perception of certain details is simply impossible. But the problem here is not any technical deficiency with recording hardware; it is simply a function of what the piano can do in generating dense sonic effects that mask many of the details contained therein. In this sense the published transcription of the Cologne improvisation is in places either a best guess or an attempt to create a performing version of the music. In other words, it employs a notational form that will create roughly the same effect without actually trying to emulate exactly the complexity of the original.

The second major phase of Part IIa begins at 7'57" as the final chord from the previous section is sustained and left to die away. This passage begins as a quiet chorale with sustained chords, and it develops gradually through melodic and textural expansion. The harmonic process this passage follows is interesting to consider. Jarrett moves through chains of diatonic chords in a manner that creates long sequences that never quite resolve but shift into different tonal regions. A useful way of considering how this works is by examining the progressions not in terms of chord function but in the lines that the treble and bass notes create as the chords move.

KEITH JARRETT'S *THE KÖLN CONCERT*

EXAMPLE 6.6   Chorale Passage, 7'57"

In Example 6.6 there is a simplified version of the opening of this passage. What becomes clear is the importance of voice leading in the construction of this progression. The first phrase is characterized by three descending melodic lines in the top voice, with the bass note generally moving in contrary motion. Subsequently, the melodic motion becomes more elaborate while retaining the overall shape of descent. This construction of the sequence results in a progression that is diatonic but does not have the kinds of harmonic movement one might expect in a jazz standard. One of the other consequences of this kind of construction is that the note in the top voice is sometimes closely connected to the sonority below (as when, on the third chord, it is the fifth), but on other occasions it is more distantly related, as when it is the ninth, or the sharpened eleventh in one instance. The effect is of a subtle fluctuation from one chord to another, in how the top voice is placed as part of the sonority below.

It is tempting to suggest that it is this voice leading in the top and bottom voices that effectively generates the harmony.[9] More important are the implications of the kind of sound this chorale passage creates. It is, as with other passages I have discussed, diatonic, but it avoids any sense of a stable harmonic center (that is, other than the first phrase, where D minor functions this way via an Aeolian modality). The changing role of the top voice in relation to the chords, sometimes as part of the triad, at other times as an upper extension, creates a subtle fluidity to the progression. It is possible to sense a shifting of diatonic areas, for instance when Jarrett begins using sharp-side pitches, moving away from the D minor/F major.

Coupled to this series of harmonic progressions, Jarrett introduces a simple motive as shown in the first two bars of Example 6.7, played in the tenor register. This figure is set against the progression of the chorale, and the motif follows the harmony (as at 8'35"), transposed through a number of levels. This begins a gradual shift, whereby the chorale texture gives way to a more active figuration in which the primary interest is melodic. As the texture builds, so the motif in the left hand is joined by

EXAMPLE 6.7   Motivic Development, Part IIa

antiphonal exchanges in the right hand, as in Example 6.7 at 9'42". Then at 10'34" the right-hand activity intensifies. In the midst of these textures the chorale movement is still perceptible, with the harmony changing at the same rate.

This intensification continues and begins to affect the left hand as well. Instead of the sustained chords, the left hand becomes increasingly active and dissonant. As shown in Example 6.7, at 11'42" this leads to declamatory right-hand octaves, set against left-hand chords that, by shifting up and down by a half-step, create a dissonant effect, further blurring the earlier harmonic clarity. Although there is a strong melodic discourse in this passage, it is not melodic development that is the primary expressive force in this passage. Instead it is texture that seems most important, given how the melodic idea is worked through different harmonic contexts as it is developed contrapuntally and antiphonally. The fixation on one melodic fragment results in a considerable textural expansion, from the simple chorale to the dense piano textures at 11'42".

Jarrett moves out of what has become quite dissonant music at 12'13" into a ballad passage beginning on E minor. This winds its way through a set of typical Jarrett chord changes into a brief phase in A♭. This particular key will become significant later on in the improvisation, so at

EXAMPLE 6.8   Reduction, 13'21"

this point it is worth noting how this A♭ area marks a brief moment of harmonic stasis. The passage follows much the same trajectory as the previous phase: a gradual thickening of texture, and increasing dissonance, leading to streams of chords that even though not dissonant in themselves are set in nonfunctional progressions. We can find typical indications of how Jarrett uses fairly standard diatonic progressions in order to create a highly mobile harmonic effect. Example 6.8 illustrates one of these passages, with the melody presented along with chord symbols indicating the harmony. Here we see a series of V-I progressions linked together by stepwise motion and thirds; the passage then goes on to delay a cadence into A♭ by way of a number of chords suspended over a D in the bass. This embedding of chained V-I progressions connected by a variety of means is what Steven Termini identifies as the "Jarrett circle of fifths," as I mentioned in Chapter Four.[10] Here, as elsewhere, in Jarrett's music this device serves to generate rapid harmonic motion which moves through diatonic areas without establishing a tonal center.

Just a little later in the passage, the harmonic motion becomes even more rapid, by way of descending parallel chords in quavers, as shown in Example 6.9. From 14'25" these chords descend into the lower registers, before making an ascent leading to a pause on some ethereal high-register sonorities. This last phase marks the most dissonant point of the whole recording, but a closer look reveals that the construction of the passage shown in Example 6.9 is actually quite straightforward. Segmenting the passage in terms of modal derivation reveals that the first three bars all shift modal orientation on the downbeat, heading toward the sharp side before the move to E♭ melodic minor. The dissonance is created in part by the fact that these shifts from one mode to another never allow the ear to adjust. Seen this way, the device that generates this kind of music is easily explainable, even if the sonic effect is quite dissonant in context.

EXAMPLE 6.9   Modal Templates as used in Part IIa

"KÖLN PART IIB"

As I have already explained, "Part IIb" follows directly on from "Part IIa," but for ease of use I will retain this demarcation used on both the LP and CD releases. This part begins, as did the previous one, with a long groove passage, this time in F# minor. Harmonically this is rather different from the earlier passages, mainly by virtue of being in a minor key. It is given a distinctive hue through the use of the flattened sixth (D), creating an F# Aeolian modality. As shown in Example 6.10, after the initial two bars, the vamp settles into a pattern with the inside voice articulating a B/C# dyad against the left hand. Although this gives the harmony a suspended-fourth sound, the Aeolian inflections and the A pitches in the right hand define the harmony as minor. In the opening stages, Jarrett uses a D major and C# minor chord at one point, implying that the vamp may become a three-chord sequence; ultimately this proves not to be the case and F# minor dominates throughout. This is again a reminder that vamp passages often go through an initial phase of stabilization before a clear accentual and harmonic pattern emerges. This vamp fits into a specific type I discussed in Chapter Four, defined by both minor key and quartal harmonic construction. The quartal element is not quite as clear as in the instances I examined previously, but the use of the B as an inner voice in preference to, and often instead of, the A that would be the minor third inflects the harmony quartally.

As with other vamps, it takes a little while before this particular passage settles down into a clear accentual framework in the manner I have

EXAMPLE 6.10   Opening to Part IIb

EXAMPLE 6.11   Accental Pattern, Opening Part IIb

previously described. When it does, as shown in Example 6.11, the emphasis leans heavily toward the second and third beats. Although the first beat of the bar is always clearly articulated, it is the push, the last sixteenth-note of the bar that is more strongly punctuated.

I have already described the kinds of phases Jarrett groove passages tend to employ, so by way of summary Table 6.1 presents the phases through which this passage develops.

TABLE 6.1   Structure of Vamp, Opening Part IIb

0'00"   Opening statement (F♯ minor Aeolian, including some use of D and C♯ minor)

0'53"   Vamp stabilizes on F♯ minor drone, with right-hand melodic improvisation

3'13"   New right-hand theme in octaves, leading to right-hand melodic improvisation over vamp

4'55"   Vamp stripped back to figuration, no melodic content

5'25"   Melodic idea from 3'13" returns, and harmony now incorporates D and C♯ minor

6'09"   Vamp stripped back, bass note drops out; transition

It is possible to see the vamp passage as flanked by two phases in which D major and C# minor are used as adjuncts to F minor. The phase beginning at 3'13" is a clear instance of the simple-complex head-solo template, in which a theme is presented in strident octaves, followed by a long right-hand improvisation over the vamp, before the theme returns once again. What is also interesting is that the transition, discussed below, is foreshadowed by an episode at 4'55" where the vamp is stripped back to bare figuration, without any melodic elaboration or thematic material at all.

When Jarrett moves on from this vamp passage, he does so via a different kind of transition from those we have seen earlier. At around 6'05" he thins the vamp down to its essential material: an oscillating right-hand A/C# and a left-hand broken chord pattern, then stopping the left hand at 6'36" in favor of an F#/E oscillation. This creates a motoric repetitive figure, which seems reminiscent of minimalist music. The transition from the vamp to this passage emphasizes continuity rather than disjuncture. Instead of abruptly leaving the vamp for new material or effecting a transition that breaks down harmonic or rhythmic continuity, the emphasis here is on transforming the vamp material in order to move into a new area.

This passage then proceeds by introducing sustained bass notes under this figuration, while moving through a series of harmonic shifts, then superimposing a simple melodic figure above it. These harmonic shifts work via a kind of premise unlike some of the harmonic strategies I outlined earlier. Present throughout this passage is the sixteenth-note motion in the inner voices. As seen from the reduction in Example 6.12, the B/C# oscillation continues for some time while the harmony changes underneath. The result is a set of chords that might otherwise seem disconnected and unrelated but make sense because they are held together by the B/C# figure. The harmonic effect maintains its interest because of how the B and C# function in different contexts. For instance, when Jarrett plays a G major harmony underneath, the B is the major third but the C# the sharpened fourth; the former pitch is consonant, the latter slightly dissonant. Similarly, on an F# harmony the B is the fourth, the C# the fifth, so both notes are strongly consonant. But on an F major harmony, the B is the sharpened fourth, the C# the sharpened fifth, so both notes are dissonant.

As Example 6.12 shows, the descending bassline is mirrored by the way in which the top line traces a series of descents, each one starting higher than the last. As with the chorale passage from Part IIa, it is as if the harmony is driven by voice leading. This first phase sets up both a

EXAMPLE 6.12   Harmonic Reduction, Part IIb, 6'36"

localized descent in melodic line and a larger-scale ascent that becomes important to the overall direction of this passage. The first large phase reaches its first peak at 8'22", by which time the right-hand line has ascended from the G_4 shown to A_5. This gradual melodic ascent is coupled with a filling out of the texture. There is, throughout this passage, a series of textural expansions taking place, of which this melodic ascent is one, as illustrated by Example 6.13.

My use of the terms "ascents" and "descents" alludes to how the shapes of these phases are articulated by expansions and contractions in dynamics, register, and texture. The music increasingly moves away from the kind of sequential harmonic movement found at its outset, to a more conventional kind of articulation of harmony. The oscillations between two notes indicated at the start of Example 6.12 gradually expand until they become a kind of broken chord left-hand figuration. This whole passage follows a long, expressive trajectory whereby it moves from that tightly clustered formation I have described in Example 6.12, to expansive piano figuration that is reminiscent of a Romantic piano style.

As the passage progresses, A^b emerges as a significant harmonic area. Both in the passage from 13'34" and earlier from 11'22", there is a considerable amount of music that stays anchored in Ab. The Ab harmony retains a highly distinctive Lydian inflection via the sharpened fourth (D), which also connects to the F$^\#$ vamp passage at the start of Part IIb. That Lydian inflection is important, as it not only firms up the connection between the two A^b passages but suggests the possibility of listeners making the same connection. The significance of A^b becomes even clearer after the passage beginning at 13'34", which gradually subsides onto a chorale like progression, outlining a I-vi-IV progression in A^b, as shown in Example 6.14 (14'08").

EXAMPLE 6.13   Phases from Part IIb

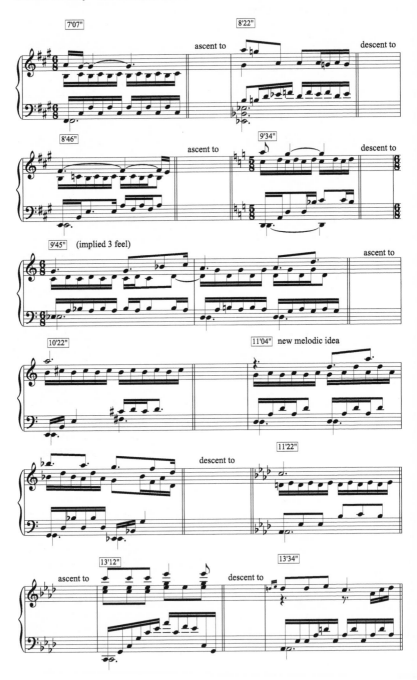

KEITH JARRETT'S *THE KÖLN CONCERT*

EXAMPLE 6.14   Chorale Episode, 14'08"

This chorale quickly becomes a heavily articulated sequence, with strong, pounding left-hand harmonies, against which Jarrett's right hand soars in fast and intricate scalic passages, recalling the rhapsodic music of Part I. Though this does seem like a new episode, the A^b tonality forms a kind of harmonic bridge to the previous passage. Then at around 15'07" the music seems to pause on a D^b sonority outlined by the left hand, while the right hand plays what appear to be fragmentary melodic ideas. This kind of musical "freeze frame" serves the expressive function of moving toward a stasis, primarily harmonically, with the left hand articulating D^b major and nothing else. This D^b major has a prominent G included, effectively still serving as the IV chord of A^b. The whole of this closing passage articulates D^b major and nothing else, but it is simultaneously poised to resolve to A^b, the implied tonality. The move toward stasis is rhythmic in the sense that articulation of the D^b harmony happens in a pulseless way, while the right-hand lines never actually establish a clear metric framework. What is most active throughout this passage is the melodic voice—but this activity is never thematic in nature. At 16'19" Jarrett sounds the final Db chord; for the remaining fifty seconds that chord is left to sustain while the right hand continues, finally moving toward a close at 16'54". This sonic move toward stasis through a long sustain reinforces the expressive idea of activity subsiding, a kind of winding down to rest.

PART II: STRUCTURAL CONSIDERATIONS

As before, it is worth considering the whole of Part II in structural terms by reviewing the kind of episodic demarcation I have suggested. For ease of use, in Table 6.2 timings are included as per the track listing, so that timings start from zero again in Part IIb.

As with Part I, what seems to emerge is a large-scale expressive contrast between groove passages (at the beginning of both Parts IIa and IIb), and the passages that follow, which in each case move through wide-ranging harmonic and textural territory. Yet there is a clear sense that the

TABLE 6.2   Structure of Köln, Part IIa and IIb

Time	Part	Tonality	Description
0'00"	**Vamp**	D major	
4'34"	Breakdown, back to vamp		
5'50"	Breakdown, back to vamp		
7'09"	Transition		
7'57"	**Chorale/ expansion**	D minor area	Expanding texturally
11'24"		F# minor (briefly)	Right-hand theme in octaves
12'13"	**Ballad**	E minor (briefly)	
12'54"		Ab pedal	
13'21"		Modulating	Becoming increasingly dissonant and dense
14'04'			Chains of descending chords, then ascending to:
14'36"			Pause on high-register chords
(Part IIb) 0'00"	**Vamp**	F# minor	(see Table 6.1)
6'09"	Transition		
6'37"	**Repetitive**	F# minor at outset, then moving through a series of keys	Oscillating sixteenth notes, broadening gradually
8'12"			Increasingly expansive piano figuration
11'22"		Ab major (Lydian) briefly	Settling onto a single harmony, before expanding once again
13'34"		Ab major (Lydian)	Settling onto Ab again
14'08"	**Chorale/coda**	Ab major	Chorale figuration gives way to rhapsodic right lines
15'07"		Db (Lydian)	Right-hand lines over sustained Db sonority

harmonically static music dominates, or at least exerts more of a pull. The most unstable passages are in the middle sections of these improvisations, and they always revert to a harmonic and rhythmic stability. This is not necessarily typical of Jarrett's improvisations from this time. Very many of the solo concerts from the 1975 tour go through a greater number of differing sections or changes of mood than the Cologne performance does. The overall effect, then, is that in Cologne Jarrett seems to foreground these vamp-based, harmonically static, rhythmically repetitive aspects of his playing more than he does in other performances.

PART IIC

Part IIc of *The Köln Concert* can be clearly differentiated from the other improvisations for good reason. This track is the encore Jarrett performed that night at the Cologne Opera House, although it is not listed as such. ECM does seem to have released Part IIc as a promotional disc, listed for "Radio Programming Only," on which the track is clearly labeled as "Encore from The Köln Concert."[11] By 1975 Jarrett had, for some time, been performing his own compositions as encores, instead of improvising complete pieces. This is certainly true of other performances from the same tour. Both the Kronach and Paris performances from the 1975 tour close with a version of "In Your Quiet Place," a ballad Jarrett had composed and recorded for the album *Keith Jarrett with Gary Burton* (1970). The Bremen concert closes with a version of "Treasure Island," the title track of an album Jarrett made for the Impulse label the previous year, as does the Freiburg concert. In these cases, the pieces performed as encores had already been recorded by Jarrett, and might have been known to members of the audience. But the case of Part IIc of the Cologne performance is rather more complicated.

During the 1970s, a publication called *The Real Book* emerged from Boston, compiled by students at the Berklee College of Music. The publication was a compilation of lead sheets of commonly played jazz compositions, and even though it was at the time technically illegal, since then the "fake book" industry has grown enormously. *The Real Book* contained a composition entitled "Memories of Tomorrow" and credited to Jarrett, which listed the recorded source as Jarrett's *The Köln Concert*. This might suggest that the tune was transcribed and given the title from the recording by a person or persons unknown. A number of bootleg recordings exist, reported by Olivier Bruchez and Maurizio Garbolino among others, which predate the Cologne performance and contain versions of what is unquestionably the same tune. The earliest seem to be a couple of trio recordings from Europe in 1966, while the tune also appears on the recording of Jarrett's 1970 solo performance in Paris discussed in Chapter One.

The question then becomes where the title "Memories of Tomorrow" could have originated, and why it was not provided on the track listing for *The Köln Concert*. There are some Jarrett encores in existence that have never been given names but that are clearly pre-composed. The encore to the 1973 Bremen concert from *Solo Concerts* is one such instance. As is well known, that encore reappears at the end of the Tokyo performance from 1984 released on video as *Last Solo*. The same piece also appears embedded within the 1972 Stockholm solo performance, as I have already mentioned in Chapter One, among the first solo concerts Jarrett performed in Europe.[12]

It is worth bearing in mind that Jarrett studied at the Berklee College of Music, and a number of his compositions besides "Part IIc" found their way into *The Real Book*. These included "Semblence" (*Facing You*), some of the tunes from the album with Gary Burton including "In Your Quiet Place," as well as "Coral." This last tune was never recorded by Jarrett but was played by Burton on his 1973 album *New Quartet*. The connection Jarrett had with Boston makes it quite possible he had composed a tune entitled "Memories of Tomorrow" that was in circulation on the Boston scene, and that he subsequently happened to perform it as the encore to the Cologne concert.

The situation is made even clearer through some correspondence that jazz scholar Barry Kernfeld reports. In a letter posted on his website, one of the original compilers of *The Real Book* (who remains anonymous) writes, "Knowing and having contacts to many famous jazz recording artists (Gary Burton, Pat Metheny, Paul Bley, Keith Jarrett, Chick Corea, Steve Swallow, etc.), we had access to first-hand material that enabled us to create an important and very useful collection of tunes."[13] This suggests that the compilers of *The Real Book* might have had access to some unrecorded Jarrett compositions. Another clue as to the origin of the title comes from a similar publication called *The Real Vocal Book*. This book seems to have come from the same origin as *The Real Book* and is certainly compiled in the same. This source has "Memories of Tomorrow" with a lyric, credited in the sheet music to "S Cornfield." Cornfield may be the same "S.C." alluded to in the introductory pages as one of the people who helped in the compilation of the book.

All of this makes it most likely that the composition was entitled "Memories of Tomorrow" before it was performed as part of the Cologne concert. As to why it was not called that on the original recording, this may simply have been part of the penchant Jarrett and Eicher had for naming solo concert improvisations in the most matter-of-fact way possible. One means of establishing the status of *The Real Book* version of "Memories of Tomorrow" is to compare it to what Jarrett actually plays on "Part IIc." If the lead sheet version were compiled solely from *The Köln Concert* recording, then it should be a reasonably consistent match to the music. There are two main factors to bear in mind in this comparison, namely the melodic and harmonic characteristics as on the lead sheet, and those as played on the recording. For the most part, harmonically the two are highly consistent. Jarrett creates a certain amount of localized variation from one chorus to another on the recording. In some instances, for example, he interjects a G minor chord between an A^b major and an F minor chord, establishing a descending sequence, while in other choruses he does not. Such localized variations can be heard as embellishments of the underlying sequence, merely decorating the underlying structure.

There is one respect in which "Part IIc" of *The Köln Concert* differs from the "Memories of Tomorrow" lead sheet. Example 6.15 shows the two relevant passages side by side. Here I have resolved two differing metrical interpretations for the purposes of comparison: the Jarrett-approved transcription interprets this piece in a fairly relaxed two-beat feel, while the lead sheet from *The Real Book* has the piece in a rather fast four. The issue of metrical interpretation is not particularly important, but what is interesting is Jarrett's turnaround between choruses. Consistently in the Cologne recording he uses an E^7 dominant, both two-thirds of the way through the tune and at its end, as a way of moving to the A minor of the start of the chorus. This happens on every chorus of the performance, allowing us to believe that this is a fairly stable feature of the composition. But on the lead sheet at both points this is indicated as a

EXAMPLE 6.15   Comparison of "Memories of Tomorrow" lead sheet with "Part IIc"

Real Book leadsheet

Part IIc, *The Köln Concert*

Bm^7–B^{b7} turnaround. In harmonic terms this is not particularly unusual, given that the B^{b7} and E^7 harmonies can be seen as interchangeable by way of what is known as the tritone substitution. But if the lead sheet had been derived solely from *The Köln Concert* recording as has sometimes been presumed, then why would the compiler have inserted a turnaround that differs from the sequence Jarrett plays on the record? The turnaround on the lead sheet is the more complex of the two versions, as it is a tritone substitution for E^7, the dominant of A minor, the simpler option and the one Jarrett actually chooses in the Cologne performance. This single disparity demonstrates that *The Real Book* compilers must have had a source for their lead sheet other than the Cologne recording. Given that Jarrett had not recorded this tune, at least on any commercial release, the source must have been either a private recording or another lead sheet, possibly one of Jarrett's own. The rendition of the tune from the 1970 Paris recording incorporates the Bm^7-B^{b7} progression, which perhaps indicates that at some point in playing the tune Jarrett came to change his mind about this turnaround.

The melodic aspect of Jarrett's rendition of the tune is rather more straightforward. Although the melody is always present, one interesting aspect of its presentation is the way it does not always appear in the uppermost voice, but also underneath an upper line of sustained pitches. Indeed the transcription uses a series of horizontal lines to pick out the motion of the melody, when on paper it is not actually clear which are the most significant pitches in the texture. Jarrett's performance of the piece on the recording is relatively straightforward. He plays the tune through twice before embarking on a short solo at 1'14" for two choruses, then restating the tune at 2'27". This is followed by a coda like passage where the music slows, before one more statement of the tune in a highly sentimental fashion. This transforms the piece from a medium-tempo Latin number into a ballad, serving as a highly expressive end to the performance. There are certainly other examples of solo concert encores in much the same vein: his rendition of "Somewhere Over the Rainbow" from the 1995 *La Scala* recording comes to mind.

The origin of "Part IIc" is one question, but there is another issue here, regarding how this piece would have been heard without the knowledge that it was composed. Given that the track listing does not signal the piece's status as a composition in the way we might expect, and also given that *The Real Book* emerged from Boston only in 1975, listeners in the 1970s would probably not have had any reason to suspect that "Part IIc" was a pre-composed piece. The question here is whether this matters or not. Does it actually make a difference whether this piece was an impromptu improvisation or a composition that Jarrett had played many times before? There are many who think it does not, who regard such debates as mere academic hair splitting. But my contention is that it does matter very much indeed, not so much because of the documentary facts themselves but because the way we hear this music is so heavily conditioned by preconceptions about composition and improvisation. The fact is that value judgments come into play very easily. A simply crafted piece of music that is improvised can be seen as more impressive than if it were composed. This is borne out by some of the remarks on the internet made by Jarrett fans about "Part IIc," which often start from the assumption that it is completely improvised. The judgment here involves a privileging of the spontaneity of improvised creation over what can be said to be the more considered drawn-out process of composition. This kind of binary opposition is deeply flawed, not least because many improvisers prepare for what they do, and many composers create musical fragments or even whole pieces with the same speed as improvisers. But the fact remains that these two labels hold much power in influencing the value we assign to a piece of music. The presumption that the lead sheet must have followed the recording is in part a demonstration of this valuing. To hear "Part IIc" as an improvisation is to acknowledge the possibility that an improviser such as Jarrett can spontaneously create something that sounds like a song form, which of course it is. In other words, an improvisation comes to bear the structural qualities of a composition, while retaining the cachet of being improvised.

The question of "Part IIc" prompts a wider one I have not yet posed; it concerns the status of the Cologne performance as an improvisation. I have suggested that a large part of this music's cultural value comes from a set of ideas about improvisation that became associated with Jarrett and his work. But this is not to say that questions about how an improviser creates music night after night, as Jarrett did on the 1975 tour, should not be brought into play. Jarrett has been keen to suggest that the solo concerts involved an approach to playing that demanded he have no ideas in his mind before starting. Writing in 1979, critic Jim Aikin suggested that in his experience of sitting in a Jarrett sound check and hearing the following concert performance, there were definite similarities: "He has ideas in the afternoon, or in the middle of the night...and he stores them at the back of this mind and hauls them out the next time he's sitting at the piano. There happen to be a lot of people listening, and he's extremely good at it. But the process is not especially mysterious."[14] Aikin's anecdotal account implies a reality rather different from the way Jarrett explains his approach.

There are occasions where passages in solo concerts from around this time make appearances in other contexts. The opening to the 1976 Kyoto concert in Japan (from *Sun Bear Concerts*) has a singularly memorable opening built on a repetitive eighth-note figure suspended above a C pedal, over which Jarrett superimposes a poignant descending melodic line.[15] And yet, in the opening to a performance from September 1976 in Frankfurt by Jarrett's European quartet, during a long piano introduction Jarrett plays exactly the same passage. The Kyoto concert followed on November 5. It is clear, then, that the opening passage to the Kyoto concert existed prior to Jarrett playing it. Whether or not it existed prior to the Frankfurt performance is another question.[16]

The January/February 1975 tour throws up an even more complex example, first pointed out by Maurizio Garbolino. The second half of the Freiburg solo concert begins with a distinctive solo melody, then joined by a spare accompaniment. As Garbolino points out, this theme is exactly the same as one recorded on the 1976 *Survivor's Suite* record, where it appears some twenty minutes into the first part. Then, in the Paris performance, recorded just under two weeks after the Freiburg concert, Jarrett begins the second half again with exactly the same theme. The reality of exactly what is going on here is impossible to determine. It could be that this theme was a piece Jarrett had been working with and used in two solo concerts, one that then went on to form part of a large suite for his American Quartet. Or it could be that its first appearance in a solo concert was genuinely as an improvisation, which was then repeated and shaped into a composition. Such speculation is interesting, but ultimately futile. What is significant is that material from one solo concert, whether it existed prior to the concert or not, is repeated in another.

It might be tempting to use this as ammunition with which to attack Jarrett's pronouncements on the originality and spontaneity of what he does in solo performance. However, I think it is much more sensible to retain a pragmatic view of such things. For Jarrett, playing night after night in European cities, attempting to come up with completely new material on every occasion, it might seem natural to ease himself into an improvisation with a piece or sequence he had previously used, which was familiar enough to function as a platform from which to explore new material.[17] This reinforces one of the arguments of this book: the solo concerts can be understood as a series of self-contained pieces, which also function as parts of large-scale improvisations. An almost impossible assumption we sometimes make about improvisation regards its distinction from composition. There is a tendency to view the two as polar opposites, in terms not only of what they say about the act of creation but also a set of aesthetic markers. Improvisation comes to stand for the spontaneous, the physical, the unconsidered, while composition is intellectual, considered, and aspiring to the quality of the masterpiece.[18] As Bruno Nettl pointed out in a famous 1974 article, a more productive way of considering this relationship is to think of composition and improvisation as existing at the ends of a continuum.[19]

The fact that Jarrett reuses material between performances does not mean this is not improvised music, nor that Jarrett is composing pieces he then uses in these improvisations. Rather, this emphasizes the essentially dialogic relationship between these two creative processes. Put in a more radical way, it reveals that the idea of these two concepts as unconnected and essentially different creative acts is profoundly misplaced. After all, it is clear that the very idea of improvisation is a Western one, as is the tendency to valorize composition over improvisation.[20] All along I have been suggesting that improvisation is an enormously important concept for the reception and understanding of Jarrett's music, as it signifies a set of ideas about music making, creativity, and artistry. But improvisation is as much a set of ideas about music making as it is about the reality of how music is actually made. It introduces modes of listening and understanding, and it leads us to make certain assumptions when we listen to music.

CHAPTER 7

TELLING THE HISTORY of a record like *The Köln Concert* is no easy task, especially if that history is about not just the making of the record but the way in which it has been received and listened to. I have already suggested something about the audience of the 1970s who might have bought and listened to it. But equally, by the acknowledgment of Manfred Eicher, and to judge by the available statistics, the record sold slowly but steadily.[1] It may have sold a considerable number of copies during the 1970s, but those sales continued into the 1980s and beyond. As I have already argued, sales figures say next to nothing of value about how a record comes to function culturally. Charting the cultural significance of *The Köln Concert* requires not statistics but a highly mobile approach that looks for contexts in which we can see values and ideas being ascribed to the recording.

With that in mind, the account I present in this chapter is a rather unconventional reception history. It is unconventional because I am interested not only in responses to the record but in how it came to be appropriated and used for a variety of purposes. Jarrett has expressed ambivalence about the recording and its ubiquity, an ambivalence that stems not just from its popularity but from what it has come to mean in relation to what is sometimes termed New Age music. This is a connotation many jazz fans find rather unpalatable, and it takes the recording far away from the context in which Jarrett would like it to be heard. Nonetheless, this association is an important part of the history of this recording and underlines the ceding of control that happens when a musician releases a record. In many senses it ceases to belong to them and is freely available for a range of uses other than those originally intended.

JARRETT AND NEW AGE MUSIC

All in all I consider that last concert probably one of the best I've ever played [the 1984 Tokyo concert from the *Last Solo* video]. In a way I'm sorry it's not on record. But in a way I'm glad too, because then what would people do? If they liked it as much as the Köln Concert…you know, people would come and say, "Hey yeah, it's really great! I've bought five of 'em so far, I wear 'em out, 'cause when I go around doing the house cleaning I like to…." Okay, go listen to George Winston, I think you'll be in good hands.[2]

The quotation above reveals Jarrett's discomfort at what the Cologne recording has come to mean for some listeners. This unease is voiced through the telling of an anecdote about a fan recounting to him a personal experience, with Jarrett's tone, even on paper, laden with dismissive sarcasm. This reaction is also expressed through the reference to pianist George Winston, along with an attempt by Jarrett to distance himself from Winston's music. These two references—to his music being used as accompaniment for the mundane domestic chore of housework, and to a fellow pianist—are closely connected. In order to see how this might be and what the implications are for understanding *The Köln Concert*, it is necessary to explore the idea of New Age music, with which Winston has been strongly associated.

Even in the early part of the twentieth century, the term New Age was being used on occasion within the Theosophist tradition.[3] Jarrett's links to this tradition, and specifically to the teachings of G. I. Gurdjieff and his disciple P. D. Ouspensky, are well known and worth exploring briefly in order to establish something more about the nature of Jarrett's belief system. According to Carr, Jarrett encountered Gurdjieff's writing while with Charles Lloyd.[4] He was not the only musician of his time to find the

Gurdjieff teachings highly relevant. According to Stuart Nicholson, pianist Mike Nock's group The Fourth Way was directly inspired by Ouspensky's writings.[5] The title of Jarrett's 1973 album *Fort Yawuh* is an anagram of "Fourth Way," one of the key terms of the Ouspensky/Gurdjieff teachings.[6] The musical results of Jarrett's involvement in this tradition seem to be confined to the *G. I. Gurdjieff Sacred Hymns* record made in 1980. But there are many hints that the influence on his music making runs much deeper, in ways that may not be immediately obvious. Beyond the *Fort Yawuh* record, other titles seem to be direct references to these teachings. There is "The Magician in You" from *Expectations* (1971), "magician" being a term Gurdjieff seems to have used to describe himself. The album of organ improvisations *Hymns/Spheres* (1976) includes pieces entitled "Hymn of Remembrance" and "Hymn of Release," titles that seem related to those of the Gurdjieff hymns Jarrett recorded, such as "Hymn to the Endless Creator" and "Hymn from a Great Temple."

But the nods Jarrett made to these teachings go far beyond the mere naming of pieces. The Gurdjieff hymns he recorded in 1980 formed an important part of these teachings. Gurdjieff dictated them to the Russian composer Thomas De Hartmann, who was a part of his circle for many years, such that in the 2002 Schott editions they are jointly credited to Gurdjieff and De Hartmann.[7] The pieces came to form an accompaniment to the repetitive ritual movements that Gurdjieff's students practiced, especially at the institute he established near Paris during the 1920s.[8] The act of recording this music was not simply a musical homage. It could be read to imply an engagement in the processes that Gurdjieff had his students undertake as part of their involvement in "the work." There is also an undoubted conceptual link between these teachings and the manner in which Jarrett conceived of the solo concerts. Christopher Chase has suggested that "Jarrett's solo performances are his parallel of the Gurdjieffian dances or movements designed to shift consciousness—not only for Jarrett, but for the entire audience as well—hence the risk. . . . These performances as a whole are far better understood as a form of occult liturgy rather than secular jazz improvisation."[9] Indeed, as I suggested in Chapter Two, certain elements of the reception of Jarrett's solo concerts during the 1970s played heavily on the idea that they were special mystical events. This is not to imply that Jarrett's music was appropriated as New Age solely because of the belief system he articulated. Jarrett never made special claims for his music in the way that some practitioners of New Age music would have at the time. But there were a range of factors, both musical and philosophical, that perhaps contributed to the appropriation of his music in these terms.

Contemporary accounts of the New Age movement in the latter part of the twentieth century stress the sheer pluralism of ideas that can be said to exist under this vast umbrella.[10] This diversity is such as to imply that the term itself can be almost meaningless, except to indicate a belief system that might be said to be esoteric or exotic, at least in its divergence from the norm. Toward the end of the 1970s and into the early 1980s, the term began to be applied to a specific kind of music. The musicians and the record labels to whom the term was applied were often uncomfortable with it, and they sought to avoid its negative connotations. If there can be said to be any central unifying aesthetic premise within New Age music, it is based not on musical style but more on the idea of music as offering a range of possibilities to the individual: variously described, these might include relaxation, healing, meditation, dreaming, and so on. Naturally this was closely connected to countercultural facets visible during the 1960s and 1970s such as psychedelia and mysticism. New Age music seemed to posit a highly romanticized investment in the potential of music as therapeutic and state-altering.

By the late 1970s a number of American musicians were being labeled as creators of New Age music and seemed willing to subscribe to this idea about music's potential. Musicians such as Stephen Halpern and Iasos are good examples. For Iasos, technology was an important part of his approach, which included the use of tape loops, drones, and amplified instruments run through reverberation effects, creating enormous amounts of artificial sustain. These effects were in themselves part of this musical vocabulary, not mere accoutrements to the language. Others associated with New Age music who used electronic instruments were Europeans such as Vangelis, Brian Eno, and Andreas Vollenweider and the Japanese composer Kitaro. But there were also musicians playing acoustic instruments such as piano, guitar, and harp who were linked to New Age music.

Jazz critics and historians have for long attempted to distance jazz from other clearly related forms of music, whether termed "popular," "easy listening," "middle of the road," or some such description. This reflects an aestheticizing trend that seeks to play on difference in order to argue for jazz as an art music. The danger of such positioning is that some of jazz's relationships with these other traditions are neglected or ignored. Indeed a number of jazz musicians made recordings during the 1970s that have been appropriated as New Age, whether or not they intended this. There was Charles Lloyd, whose 1979 record *Pathless Path* for Unity Records (originally released on ADC Records) incorporated synthesizer, the Japanese koto, and a lush, often harmonically static, musical landscape.[11] The origins of this sort of approach go back much further, not least to a record identified, for example, by David Fricke in *Rolling Stone* as a kind of precursor to New Age music: Tony Scott's *Music for Zen Meditation* (1964).[12] Such records were nothing more than indications of a trend that took a number of forms, as for instance in records made during the 1960s featuring rich orchestrations coupled with undemanding improvisations by jazz musicians. Bill Evans's *Bill Evans Plays the Theme from the V.I.P.s and Other Great Songs* (1963) and Paul Desmond's *Desmond Blue* (1961) are good examples of this tendency.[13] Naturally such albums do not feature prominently, if at all, within the jazz literature, perhaps because they explicitly problematize the relationship between jazz and "middle-of-the-road" or "easy listening" music. The case of Windham Hill Records, the label credited with making pianist George Winston successful, demonstrates how such stylistic labels often disguise as much as they reveal.

Windham Hill Records was founded by guitarist William Ackermann in 1976, partly to release an album of his own guitar music. He subsequently signed a range of artists, most famously Winston. Windham Hill became known for high-fidelity recordings of acoustic music, coupled with evocative album art. The cover to Winston's best-selling record *Autumn* (1980) is a plain image of a green tree against a clear blue sky. The link is easy to make and is even supported by Ackermann's own account of going to a record shop before deciding on the cover art for his first record, and concluding that the ECM releases had the cover art that he liked the most.[14] The connection goes much deeper than just album art. As a number of writers on Windham Hill pointed out at the time, the connection with earlier precedents in jazz, not just ECM, was striking.[15] Just as European musicians had been seen to look to their own native traditions for inspiration, resulting in the development of what has sometimes been called a Nordic tone channeled through ECM, American musicians did likewise. The use of a pure diatonic harmony without alterations is an example of this process, as I discussed in Chapter Five. Also highly relevant is the music recorded by a range of American groups that, although sometimes labeled as jazz, clearly had interests going far beyond the boundaries of what many would have considered the norm stylistically. The Paul Winter Consort was an influential group in this respect, leading to an even more important offshoot group, Oregon, which included guitarist Ralph Towner and reed player Paul McCandless. Oregon's use of acoustic instruments including guitar, tabla, bass, oboe, and soprano saxophone resulted in a timbral mix that was clearly not standard for jazz. Indeed the group was well known in Germany around the time Jarrett was touring in 1975. Chuck Berg called this the "Euro-folk dimension" in a 1983 article on Windham Hill, describing how Jarrett and Chick Corea represented a similar inclination in American jazz.[16]

But there was also a side to ECM's reception in America that demonstrated that the emergence of this new tone in the jazz language was not altogether welcome. Neil Tesser's *Down Beat* review of guitarist Pat Metheny's 1977 ECM recording *Watercolors* identified the salient points in what he termed the "ECM controversy": "Critics of the label, its producer, and its distinctive sound point quickly to Metheny (along with his former employer Gary Burton and a few others) when they start moaning about white middle-class jerkwater jazz and suburban soul. He is written off as being too clean, sounding too pure: even his song titles come under icy fire."[17] The downside was that this new musical tone, allied to ECM's distinctive production aesthetics, was seen as overly bland, approaching a kind of respectability that could be negatively associated with a set of social stereotypes. This forgotten side to ECM's reception in America points to the fact that its links with Windham Hill recordings stretched beyond cover art to the utility of music.

A number of the musicians recording for Windham Hill made their connections to the jazz tradition explicit through their performances. Although Winston's performances tended to showcase his own compositions, he was also known for his interpretations of Vince Guaraldi and Professor Longhair. Jarrett's own statements on the matter seem to put clear water between his approach and that of Winston, and likewise Winston also chose to differentiate his music from Jarrett's. Winston's brand of acoustic piano music, smothered in ample amounts of artificial reverberation, creates a lush and identifiable sound, one immediately familiar as evocative of contemporary ambient soundtracks. But were Winston and Jarrett linked simply because they both performed solo piano music that happened, at times, to be highly melodic?

Winston's 1980 album *Autumn*, his first for Windham Hill, provides a good example. The opening piece from the album, "Color/Dance," is shown in Example 7.1. Here the left-hand arpeggios, played with the sustain pedal down, create a boomy resonance with a long sustain. The effect is as if the pedal is held down throughout, although much of this is achieved through the use of reverberation. The construction of the harmonies here is typical of Winston: the left hand outlines a I-ii sequence in A major, but with both harmonies having a distinctive added ninth. The pentatonic-sounding melodic gesture ascends over this rolling accompaniment. This distinctively open-sounding diatonic harmony,

EXAMPLE 7.1 George Winston, "Colors/Dance"

which I have already described as characteristic of parts of *The Köln Concert*, notably the opening, is prominent in much of Winston's music. In fact, this simple harmonic sequence cycling between two root-position chords voiced in broken figuration is the same as the G major/A minor sequence that underpins much of the first half of Part I from the Cologne recording.

Other tracks from *Autumn* demonstrate a more harmonically static style, which again is strongly reminiscent of some of Jarrett's vamp-type passages. "Woods" works with a D^b minor harmony inflected with a raised seventh degree that continues for more than two minutes until the piece progresses to a brighter E major. "Stars" starts with a left-hand pattern articulating an open D sonority that continues for most of the five-and-a-half-minute duration. Winston's approach on such pieces lacks the groove quality Jarrett creates, but the accordance between the two styles is quite clear.

But this is by no means to suggest that Winston was borrowing from Jarrett, or consciously imitating him. After all, musicians are inevitably aware of each other's work, and the fact that Winston and Jarrett should both mention one another in interviews merely reinforces this fact. Rather, it is better to understand that a certain part of Jarrett's style drew from the same source as Winston, and it was perhaps inevitable that there should be such common ground. Winston's use of a diatonic language enriched with non chromatic alterations reflected the uses musicians such as Burton, Corea, and Metheny had made of this language (earlier in the decade in some cases), while also alluding to a range of vernacular musics. Seen this way, then, *The Köln Concert* may, perhaps, have served to demonstrate the commercial potential of such a musical language.

THE KÖLN CONCERT *AS A NEW AGE RECORD*

By 1980, a company called Unity Records was advertising its catalogue of "New Age Music" in publications such as *Yoga Journal*, listing Jarrett among artists including Eno, Halpern, Iasos, Jordan de la Sierra, and Paul Horn.[18] Of the artists mentioned in the advertisement, some can be immediately identified with New Age music in the sense of a conscious aesthetic to create music with transcendental properties—Iasos and Halpern in this case. Others, such as Eno and Horn, would probably not have labeled themselves as new age; Eno certainly described his work at this time using the moniker "ambient." Some of these artists would have been recording for Unity Records, but others, including Jarrett, were not, and so presumably Unity was simply acting as a retailer. Nonetheless, the fact that a record label associated with the more mystical end of New Age should have been listing Jarrett in this manner is significant. The question this prompts is probably obvious: Why? Certainly the way Jarrett saw his music would be radically different from the case of some of the artists promoted by Unity Records. The answer, I believe, is because of how *The Köln Concert* was coming to be used by listeners, alluded to by the quotation I used earlier about the recording functioning as a soundtrack to housework.

The idea that music can be serious, or hold the status of art, is generally linked with a certain presumption about aestheticism, or how it ought to be treated. It suggests that just as one should contemplate a painting in a gallery in a considered way, not simply glancing at it and moving on, thus listening to music is something to be undertaken intentionally, and carefully. This aesthetic developed particularly during the nineteenth century in the European classical tradition and was linked to the idea that music should be performed in a concert hall. It was particularly associated with instrumental music, music that demanded attention free from the prompting of words. As Christopher Small points out, the very design of concert halls is premised on the notion that the music should communicate to the audience with as little interference or distraction as possible. In this view of music, performance is an event marked out by particular places—clubs, concert halls, and so on. These places are marked out from the rest of everyday life by their location, and by how people are expected to behave. We do not, by and large, act in the concert hall as we do in everyday life; there is a protocol involved, and the demands of etiquette, as Small explains in his book *Musicking*.[19]

Seen in this light, the advent of recorded music allows the potential for an enormously radical shift in how listeners engage with music. With sound recording, musical performance no longer has to be an event. The idea of music's repeatability via the medium of recording prompted a famous 1936 essay by Walter Benjamin, in which he described the impending era of mass reproduction as signaling the demise of the aura of the original.[20] This repeatability has allowed listeners to appropriate music and use it in contexts that artists might never have envisaged. Not only does this make it easier for music to be played in a enormous variety of contexts given the availability of playback devices such as the modern MP3 player, but it means music can signify very different things depending on the context in which it is used.

The approach taken by musicologist and sociologist Tia DeNora in her influential study *Music in Everyday Life* (2000) is that the possibilities music affords in this way cannot be understood solely by recourse to the "music itself," a phrase beloved of musicologists. Instead, DeNora works from the principle that listeners or viewers enter into cultural artefacts and put them into action in a range of ways.[21] These appropriations, or uses, of music are important for musicologists, not least in the case of recorded music, because they help to focus attention on the fact that a recording is not simply a collection of sounds but a text that is shaped by how listeners engage with it. So it is that Jarrett's wariness about the popularity of *The Köln Concert* and its use in numerous contexts might be said to reflect a resistance to such potential, to hold on to the idea of a recording as an artwork.

How does one put DeNora's ideas into action in a context such as this, when examining how listeners engage with a particular recording? Critical reviews such as those I have already referred to in Chapters One and Two do not, by and large, give us access to this kind of information. They are self-conscious pronouncements on value and merit, saying little about how listeners engage with recording. What I want to turn to here are a range of responses to *The Köln Concert*, which may appear unconventional in nature. These are not responses to the recording by critics, fans, or musicians, and they do not emanate from within what we might term a musical community. They do not, as we will see, seem to engage directly with the music itself, or even really attempt to describe it. They might seem to have nothing to do with the music, but I will argue quite the opposite.

The Köln Concert makes an appearance in a 2009 novel by Francisco X. Stork, entitled *Marcelo in the Real World*. In the book, the eponymous protagonist, who, according to the book's publicity, suffers from a kind of autistic condition whereby he can hear music no one else can hear, visits the home of his colleague Jasmine.[22] He notices a poster with the words

"Keith Jarrett, The Köln Concert" and is struck by this: "Below these words I see the black-and-white image of a man playing a piano. His eyes are closed, his head is lowered, and his chin rests on his chest. I immediately recognize the posture of someone in deep prayer. The man is playing the piano, but I am certain he is also remembering."[23] In the scene that follows, Jasmine sits at the piano and plays a short improvisation, which mesmerizes Marcelo. She describes her playing to him as "remembering," saying "it's a word I use for praying. Sometimes it's like waiting for music to come out of the silence." In this passage The Köln Concert appears through the imagery of this poster. The music of the recording remains unheard in the narrative, but it is what Jarrett and this recording stand for that is significant. Jasmine tells Marcelo she works during the day in order that she can play the piano. The equation of playing the piano here with the act of praying or remembering sets it apart as an activity that is not simply the banal act of making music, but a profound kind of introspective escape or transport. Here, The Köln Concert serves to articulate an idea about music's power, linked to a particular sort of creative aesthetic. The image of Jarrett is also present via the description of the poster, which allows the specter of Jarrett's performing body to enter into the scene, again as a symbol of a kind of creativity.

Stork's book is an unusual example of The Köln Concert making an appearance in a fictional narrative because of how the recording's aesthetic is articulated and specified. But the recording surfaces in a range of books, both fictional and otherwise—books that are not explicitly about music. These appearances serve as fragments of a complex reception history, glimpses of a much larger picture. There are many references in a number of works of fiction to The Köln Concert as a recording used for background music. In that respect it might be said to be like almost any other sound recording, mentioned just in passing. Many of these references, read carefully, say something not just about the recording, but about a history of use and appropriation.

Consider a recent example from a 2009 novel by Jane Elmor, called Pictures of You.[24] The main character, Luna, attends a funeral at which The Köln Concert is played, as it is one of the favorite pieces of the deceased. It moves her to tears because not only is it poignant in this setting but it is one of her own favorite pieces, and she paints to it. Or from Bertice Berry's novel Redemption Song (2001), in which, "In her absence Ross put on Keith Jarrett's Köln Concert, Side one. Fina smiled hearing the music—the one piece of music that could get her through anything. She studied to it in college, and cried to it when her father died."[25] Or The Song House by Trezza Azzopardi in which one of the characters puts the record on because it is "languid, summer rain music," and he hopes it will help him write.[26] In these examples the record is used as background music because it seems to afford a number of possibilities for the characters in these books.[27] The function of the recording in these cases is not to act as an object of contemplation, but to create certain moods or ideas for the characters in question. It is not so much the music on the record that these characters seek but the possibilities that the music affords, whether it be a sense of reflection, relaxation, or invocation of memory.

We can find these ideas being ascribed to the piece in a number of instances where it is recommended for functional purposes. For instance, the 1988 book *You Bring Out the Music in Me: Music in Nursing Homes* explores the potential of music used in nursing homes to help "encourage relaxation and expression of feeling and increase socialization."[28] An essay in the book by Louise Lynch provides a set of "mood music" suggestions. She lists a series of moods with corresponding suggestions of pieces that can be played in order to help set the desired mood. These moods include "Prayerful/Reverent," "Sad, Melancholy," and so on. *The Köln Concert* appears in the "Nostalgic/Sentimental/Soothing" category along with classical pieces that include Beethoven's "Moonlight" Sonata (Sonata No. 14 in C# minor), Bach's Air on the G string (the second movement of the Orchestral Suite No. 3 in D major), and recordings that might be described as New Age, such as one by Steven Halpern.[29] Similarly, Jean Houston's book *The Hero and the Goddess* (part of a genre sometimes known as "self-help") describes *The Köln Concert* as one of the pieces readers can use to create their own "sacred space."[30]

One of the appearances *The Köln Concert* makes within film soundtracks is the Nanni Moretti film *Caro Diario* (1993). In the semi autobiographical film, Moretti (who stars as well as directs) takes a trip on his scooter to the scene of the assassination of Pier Paolo Pasolini, an Italian film director and artist. Shots of Moretti riding along winding roads are accompanied by music from Part I, namely the G major–A minor episode with the rhapsodic right-hand lines. The effect is highly melancholic and bittersweet, hinting, it seems, at the deeper significance of the journey.

These instances also point to something DeNora discusses, namely the range of uses to which listeners can put music. It is worth considering how in none of these instances does *The Köln Concert* function as a musical object to be contemplated. Listeners do not sit and listen to it as one would at a concert. They use it for specific purposes, sometimes the background to specific domestic work, or for rituals (the funeral mentioned in one of the novels), or relaxation. This is, as I have already argued, a function of the way in which recording technology has transformed how we can engage with music. But these instances also link to something Jarrett alludes to in the quotation at the outset: this particular recording seems to afford another kind of use from that which we might normally expect, not simply in its link with relaxation but with the idea of poignancy, regret, and spirituality. Such uses of a recording might not conventionally be considered part of reception history, simply because they may seem peripheral to the music. Nor is it simply the fact that *The Köln Concert* has occasionally come to function in this way. Rather, there is a sense that the recording's legacy is now dominated by this idea of its functionality, and the idea of background music, and a coffee table record. It is this association that is behind both Jarrett's occasional attempts to disown the record and the suspicion with which it is treated by some jazz critics and historians. The association has built gradually over the years, fueled by the increasing currency of the idea of functional music.

CONCLUSION

At the very start of this book, I began with the sales figures for *The Köln Concert*, statistics that have been cited by many journalists. But I also posed a question about how it might be possible to go beyond statistics, to chart a record's impact not merely in terms of the commercial impact described by the number of units sold. I have been keen to suggest that this record came to stand for something, to function in variety of ways as a symbol of an idealized spontaneous creativity, an acoustic music free from the trappings of electronics. We can see at this point how those conceptions can become something rather different. The use of the record as background music emphasizes its potential functionality. The recording itself is not so important; more significant are the opportunities it affords its listeners.

These ideas demonstrate how close *The Köln Concert* has been to New Age music because of this history of usage. What lies behind many of the ascriptions of the label New Age to George Winston is the view that banal uses of music are something to which jazz should neither subscribe nor be subject. Thus, *The Köln Concert* sits on a kind of aesthetic faultline. On the one side, its invocation of the improvisatory ideal places it within a jazz tradition that valorizes the importance of the spontaneous performance over the methodical and carefully rehearsed approach, even at the risk of idealizing this aesthetic to the point of distortion. But on the other, the history of the record's associations in the 1970s as a "coffee table" item, relegating it to the status of background music, and then in some of the usages discussed previously, suggests that it is something jazz records are not expected to be.

Recordings have been the primary medium scholars use to talk about jazz, because they offer so much musical information, providing a documentation that is compelling in its immediacy. They allow us to hear the sound of the great jazz players, to hear the interactions among musicians, even to hear the mistakes, and the performances that did not quite come off. And the music of *The Köln Concert* has much to say about how Jarrett adapted his approach to the new format he created, and about how listening to improvised music creates very particular expressive effects. But what is lacking in accounts of jazz recordings is what happens when listeners take these records home and live with them. As the case of *The Köln Concert* demonstrates, records have their own complex histories, which start at the moment of their inception but which continue onward and outward, navigating complex cultural avenues. *The Köln Concert* began life as the result of an ambitious musical challenge Jarrett set himself, a challenge that said much about the cultural values of the time. But in the years since its release it has become something much more complex than just a document of a performance given on a substandard piano at a sold-out Cologne Opera House. It has accrued its own story as listeners continue to find their own meanings when they engage with it.

NOTES

NOTES TO INTRODUCTION

1. See for instance John Fordham, "50 Great Moments in Jazz: Anthony Braxton Swims Against the Tide." http://www.guardian.co.uk/music/musicblog/2011/apr/13/50-moments-anthony-braxton-jazz (July 5, 2011).

2. John Fordham, "50 Great Moments in Jazz: Keith Jarrett's The Koln Concert." http://www.guardian.co.uk/music/musicblog/2011/jan/31/50-great-moments-jazz-keith-jarrett (July 5 2011).

3. "For One Night Only", BBC Radio 4, broadcast April 9, 2011. The BBC was not the first broadcaster to create a documentary on *The Köln Concert*. In 2009 Swedish broadcaster Sveriges Radio aired a documentary called "Det Ospelbara Pianot" (The Unplayable Piano). http://sverigesradio.se/sida/artikel.aspx?programid=3493&artikel=2898256 (July 5 2011).

4. A news item on Bösendorfer's website provides a little more information about the problem with the piano on the day of the performance. "The Köln Concert." http://www.bo-esendorfer.com/en/current-news.html?page=5408 (January 25 2011). This account differs somewhat from Brandes's. The piano that had been requested was, according to her, not in the Opera house at all, and therefore could not have been brought to the stage.

5. Ian Carr, *Keith Jarrett: The Man and His Music* (London: Paladin, 1992), 70–73. "Det Ospelbara Pianot," Sveriges Radio, 2009.

6. "For One Night Only," BBC Radio, 2011.

7. See for instance Jed Rasula, "The Media of Memory: The Seductive Menace of Records in Jazz History," in *Jazz Among the Discourses*, ed. Krin Gabbard (London: Duke University Press, 1995), 136; Scott DeVeaux, "Constructing the Jazz Tradition: Jazz Historiography," *Black American Literature Forum* 25/3 (Autumn 1991): 532.

8. Evan Eisenberg, *The Recording Angel* (New Haven: Yale University Press, 2005), 89.

9. See for instance Theodore Gracyk, *Rhythm and Noise: An Aesthetics of Rock* (London: Tauris, 1996), 37–67.

10. Matthew Butterfield, "Music Analysis and the Social Life of Jazz Recordings," *Current Musicology* 71–73 (Spring 2001–Spring 2002): 332.

11. See for instance Macero's own account of the creative process involved in the production of records like *In A Silent Way*. http://milesite.blogspot.com/2009/02/teo-macero-on-producing-miles-davis.html (January 25, 2011).

12. Butterfield, "Music Analysis and the Social Life of Jazz Recordings," 332–33.

13. Philip Auslander, *Liveness: Performance in a Mediatized Culture* (London: Routledge, 1999), 3.

14. Quoted in Auslander, *Liveness*, 39.

NOTES TO CHAPTER ONE

1. See for instance Rasula, "The Media of Memory."

2. E. Taylor Atkins, ed., *Jazz Planet* (Jackson: University of Mississippi Press, 2003), xiii.

3. Ronald Radano, *New Musical Figurations: Anthony Braxton's Cultural Critique* (Chicago: University of Chicago Press, 1993), 142–48. George Lewis, *A Power Stronger Than Itself: The AACM and American Experimental Music* (Chicago: University of Chicago Press, 2008), 215–57.

4. Paul Bley, with David Lee, *Stopping Time: Paul Bley and the Transformation of Jazz* (Canada: Vehicule Press, 1999), 99–107.

5. Quoted in Ingrid Monson, *Freedom Sounds: Civil Rights Call out to Jazz and Africa* (New York: Oxford University Press, 2007), 268.

6. Jenny Armstrong, "Dexter Gordon: Transcontinental Terrorist," *Down Beat* 39/12 (June 22, 1972): 17.

7. Radano, *New Musical Figurations*, 142.

8. Mike Heffley, *Northern Sun, Southern Moon: Europe's Reinvention of Jazz* (New Haven: Yale University Press, 2005), 1–4.

9. Carr, *Keith Jarrett*, 28–39. Stuart Nicholson, *Jazz Rock: A History* (Edinburgh: Canongate, 1998), 77–82.

10. George Avakian, liner notes to Keith Jarrett, *Life Between the Exit Signs*, Vortex LP 2006, 1967.

11. Joe Klee, "Keith Jarrett, Spontaneous Composer," *Down Beat* 39/1 (January 20, 1972): 12, 36.

12. Carr, *Keith Jarrett*, 58.

13. This account has been confirmed by Manfred Eicher. Gary Giddins, "A Conversation with Manfred Eicher." http://fora.tv/2009/11/19/Jazz_A_Conversation_with_Manfred_Eicher#fullprogram (July 4, 2011).

14. Carr, *Keith Jarrett*, 61.

15. See for instance R. Shaw, "Keith Jarrett: *Shades*," *Down Beat* 44/10 (May 19, 1977): 26.

16. J. S. Roberts, "In the Middle with Jarrett," *Melody Maker* (April 12, 1975): 40.

17. Interview with Jarrett by Sara Fishko, as part of *The Fishko Files*, WNYC Radio, Wednesday, June 4, 2003. http://www.prx.org/pieces/10396-wnyc-s-fishko-files-an-hour-with-keith-jarrett (July 4, 2011). The earliest reference to the Heidelberg performance I can find is John S. Wilson writing in the *New York Times* in March 1975. That Wilson mentioned the Heidelberg performance implies that Jarrett had recounted

this story to him, or that it was part of some publicity material he was using. John S. Wilson, "Jazz Pianist to Slow Pace," *New York Times* (March 23, 1975): 80.

18. Ted Panken, "What Am I Doing," *Down Beat* 75/12 (December 2008): 37.

19. Various Artists, *Heidelberger Jazztage '72*, MPS Records, 21 21655-1, 1973.

20. Ben F. Carruthers, "Germany in '72," *Oakland Tribune* (August 13, 1972): 13, 20, 24.

21. Author unknown, "Die Einsamkeit des Paul Bley," *Jazz Podium* (July/August 1973): 10–12.

22. "For One Night Only," BBC Radio 4, 2011.

23. Ilhan Mimaroglu, "Keith Jarrett, Mercer Arts Center, New York City," *Down Beat* 40/1 (January 18, 1973): 36.

24. Bob Palmer, "Keith Jarrett, *Facing You*," *Rolling Stone* 124 (December 21, 1972): 48.

25. These pieces have been identified by Maurizio Garbolino. "Lucy in the Sky with Diamonds" was recorded on the Beatles' *Sgt. Pepper's Lonely Hearts Club Band* album, released in 1967. "Here Comes the Sun" was released in 1969 on the *Abbey Road* LP. Jarrett had told François Postif in 1969 that *Abbey Road* was one of the records he was listening to at that time. Carr, *Keith* Jarrett, 43–44.

26. Carr, *Keith Jarrett*, 65.

27. The information in this table is drawn from a number of sources, including ECM's tour brochure, and also Olivier Bruchez's website, which collates information provided by Jarrett enthusiasts. http://www.keithjarrett.org (August 1, 2011).

28. "La Selva: Organic Food in the Tuscan Tradition." http://www.ecmrecords.com/News/Diary/49_LaSelva.php?cat=&we_start=24 (July 4, 2011).

29. Though it seems likely that a review of Jarrett's Cologne performance appeared in one of the city's newspapers, I have been unable to track it down, although I am grateful to Vera Brandes for her attempts to contact various newspapers there on my behalf.

30. Bruno Rub, "The Baden Concert. Keith Jarrett's Badener Gastspiel am Tag nach dem legendären 'Köln Concert'," in *Badener Neujahrsblätter 2006* (2006): 150–56.

31. Ibid.

32. Wilson, "Jazz Pianist to Slow Pace," 80.

33. Karsten Flohr, "Jazz-Pianist Begann als Wunderkind," *Hamburger Abendblatt* (January 30, 1975): 9.

34. Karsten Flohr, "Keith Jarrett Vermittelte Zwischen Gestern und Heute," *Hamburger Abendblatt* (February 2, 1975): 23.

35. Miles Davis had brought his band to listen to Jarrett's trio playing in a Paris club, just before the trumpeter persuaded Jarrett to join his band. Carr, *Keith Jarrett*, 46.

36. Lucien Malson, "Jazz: Keith Jarrett," *Le Monde* (February 7, 1975): 28.

37. Leonard Feather, "Antibes: from Bass to Bagpipe," *Los Angeles Times* (August 11, 1974): 51.

38. Wilson, "Jazz Pianist to Slow Pace," 80.

39. Ibid.

NOTES TO CHAPTER TWO

1. Eric Porter, "Introduction: Rethinking Jazz Through the 1970s," *Jazz Perspectives* 4/1 (2010): 1.

2. Nicholson, *Jazz Rock*, xv.

3. See for instance Gary Tomlinson, "Cultural Dialogics and Jazz: A White Historian Signifies," *Black Music Research Journal* 11/12 (Autumn 1991): 229–64.

4. Nicholson, *Jazz Rock*, 29.

5. Ibid., 33.

6. John Burks, "Monterey Jazz Festival," *Rolling Stone* 21 (November 9, 1968): 14.

7. David Ake, "The Emergence of the Rural American Ideal in Jazz: Keith Jarrett and Pat Metheny on ECM," *Jazz Perspectives* 1/1 (2007): 53–55.

8. Keith Jarrett, liner notes to *Solo Concerts*, ECM 1035-37, 1973.

9. "Rolling Stone Music Awards 1973," *Rolling Stone* 152 (January 17, 1974): 11.

10. Peter M. Shane, "Rock and Folk," *Harvard Crimson* (March 7, 1974). http://www.thecrimson.com/article/1974/3/7/rock-and-folk-pbgerald-ford-and/ (July 4 2011).

11. Robert Christgau, "Our Own Critics' Poll," *Village Voice* (January 20, 1975): 103–4.

12. "Arbour Zena," *Billboard* (June 26, 1976). http://www.billboard.biz/ (November 24, 2010).

13. "Staircase," *Billboard* (June 11, 1977) http://www.billboard.biz/ (November 24, 2010).

14. James Lincoln Collier, "Jazz in the Jarrett Mode," *New York Times* (January 7, 1979): 17.

15. Bob Palmer, "Keith Jarrett: *Luminescence*," *Rolling Stone* 200 (November 20, 1975): 68, 71.

16. *Down Beat* had been trying to make an effort to move toward a wider audience under the direction of editor Dan Morgenstern, incorporating advertisements for guitar amplifiers and reviewing rock records, a move seen as symptomatic of the changing cultural times. See John Gennari, *Blowin' Hot and Cool: Jazz and Its Critics* (Chicago: University of Chicago Press, 2006), 292. Nicholson, *Jazz Rock,* 12.

17. Palmer, "Keith Jarrett: *Luminescence*," 71.

18. Juan Rodriguez, "Critic's Choice: Rock's Top Ten This Year," *Montreal Gazette* (December 26, 1975): 72.

19. Neil Tesser, "Keith Jarrett: *The Köln Concert*," *Down Beat* 42/4 (February 12, 1975): 22.

20. Steve Lake, "Jarrett: Romance Is Not Dead," *Melody Maker* (December 11, 1975): 43.

21. John S. Wilson, "In League with the Jazz Giants," *New York Times* (September 28, 1975): 399.

22. Joachim-Ernst Berendt, "Schönheit, die ich meine. Der neue Faschismus in Jazz und Rock," *Jazz Podium* (January 1976): 9–12. The article was originally published in the Swiss journal *Die Weltwoche* and was later reprinted elsewhere, including in one of Berendt's own books.

23. For a discussion of Berendt's article and specifically its argument about fascism, see Andrew Wright Hurley, *The Return of Jazz: Joachim-Ernst Berendt and West German Cultural Change* (New York: Berghahn Books, 2009), 208–11.

24. Wolfram Knauer indicates that Berendt was thinking specifically of the "quasi-religious" elements of Jarrett's solo concerts in his remarks, even though this is never made explicit. Wright Hurley, *The Return of Jazz*, 236.

25. Author unknown, "The Year's Best LPs," *Time Magazine* (December 29, 1975). http://www.time.com/time/magazine/article/0,9171,945465,00.html (August 16, 2011).

26. *Billboard* (December 25, 1976).

27. Michael Segell, "The Children of 'Bitches Brew'," *Rolling Stone* 282 (December 28, 1978): 43–47.

28. Mikal Gilmore, "Reeling in the Seventies: Jazz Tries to Cope with Success," *Rolling Stone* 295 (July 12, 1979): 53.

29. Jeremy A. Smith, "'Sell It Black': Race and Marketing in Miles Davis's Early Fusion Jazz," *Jazz Perspectives* 4/1 (April 2010): 7–33.

30. Will Layman, "Keith Jarrett: Setting Standards." http://www.popmatters.com/pm/review/keith-jarrett-setting-standards/ (July 4, 2011).

31. Carr, *Keith Jarrett*, 38.

32. Bill Quinn, "Charles Lloyd: Forest Flower," *Down Beat* 34/11 (June 1, 1967): 35.

33. Paul Tanner, "Jazz Goes to College: Part I," *Music Educators Journal* 57/7 (March 1971): 57, 105–9, 111–13. "Jazz Goes to College, Part II," *Music Educators Journal* 57/8 (April 1971): 49, 85–93.

34. Bruce Luty, "Jazz Ensembles' Era of Accelerated Growth, Part II," *Music Educator's Journal* 69/4 (December 1982): 49–50, 64.

35. David Ake, *Jazz Cultures* (Los Angeles: University of California Press, 2002), 113.

36. Peter King, "Latest Jarrett Album 'Enjoyable'," *Daily Collegian* (February 2, 1976): 7.

37. Amy Lee, "Newport Jazz Festival—Jazz?" *Chronicle Telegram/Sunday Scene* (July 18, 1976): 63.

38. Paul Scanlon, "16th Monterey Jazz Festival," *Rolling Stone* 147 (November 8, 1973): 26.

39. See for instance Bob Palmer, "Jazz/Rock '74: The Plain Funky Truth," *Rolling Stone* 166 (August 1, 1974): 16–17.

40. Leonard Feather, "Take Four: Jazz by Brubecks," *Rolling Stone* 183 (March 27, 1975): 13.

41. Ira Gitler, "Jazz on the Comeback Trail," *Family Weekly* (July 6, 1975): 10.

42. See for instance Melvin Maddocks, "Jazz Fans in Revival Mood," *Advocate* (September 20, 1975): 20.

43. Leonard Feather, "Jarrett: Harbinger of New Forms?" *Los Angeles Times* (June 14, 1976): G19.

44. John S. Wilson, "In Dancing Spirits: Jarrett Improvises on the Keyboard," *New York Times* (March 4, 1975): 41.

45. Herbert Aronoff, "Fine Pianist Plays Mystical Music," *Montreal Gazette* (October 24, 1974): 52.

46. Juan Rodriguez, "Jarrett Treats Fans to a Philosophy of Music," *Montreal Gazette* (August 30, 1979): 25.

47. On the question of Jarrett's vocalizing and bodily movements, see Jairo Moreno, "Body'n'soul: Keith Jarrett's Pianism," *Musical Quarterly* 83/1 (Spring 1999): 75–92; and Peter Elsdon, "Listening in the Gaze: The Body in Keith Jarrett's Solo Piano Improvisations," in *Music and Gesture*, eds. Elaine King and Anthony Gritten (Aldershot: Ashgate, 2006), 192–207.

48. Tony Whyton, *Jazz Icons: Heroes, Myths and the Jazz Tradition* (Cambridge: Cambridge University Press, 2010), 45.

49. Auslander, *Liveness*, 74.

50. See for instance Bill Mikowksi, "Jarrett Is Mix of Lunatic, Genius," *Milwaukee Journal* (November 19, 1977): 7.

51. Jarrett, liner notes to *Solo Concerts*.

52. Bob Palmer, "The Inner Octaves of Keith Jarrett," *Down Beat* 41/17 (October 24, 1974): 16–17, 46.

53. Palmer, "Keith Jarrett, *Facing You*," 48.

54. Christopher Small, *Musicking: The Meanings of Performing and Listening* (Hanover, NH: Wesleyan University Press, University Press of New England, 1998), 94–95.

55. Lewis Porter, "John Coltrane's *A Love Supreme*: Jazz Improvisation as Composition," *Journal of the American Musicological Society* 38/3 (1995): 593–621.

56. Radano, *New Musical Figurations*, 69–70.

57. Eric Porter, *What Is This Thing Called Jazz?* (Los Angeles: University of California Press, 2002), 241.

58. Chick Corea, "The Function of an Artist," *Down Beat* 38/18 (October 28, 1971): 16.

59. Charles Reich, *The Greening of America* (New York: Random House, 1970). Theodore Roszak, *The Making of a Counter Culture* (London: Faber and Faber, 1970).

60. Roszak, *The Making of a Counter Culture*, 147.

61. Peter Clecak, *America's Quest for the Ideal Self* (New York: Oxford University Press, 1983).

62. Bruce J. Schulman, *The Seventies: The Great Shift in American Culture, Society and Politics* (New York: Da Capo Press, 2001), 78–79.

63. See William Graebner, "America's Poseidon Adventure: A Nation in Existential Despair," in *America in the 70s*, eds. Beth Bailey and David Farber (Lawrence: University Press of Kansas, 2004), 157–80.

64. Tom Wolfe, *The Purple Decades* (London: Picador, 1993), 265–93.

65. In this respect Jarrett's posture on the cover is similar to that of Bill Evans, as discussed by David Ake, who posits that this bowed posture conveys "deep thought, profound piety, or heartfelt sadness." Ake, *Jazz Cultures*, 98.

66. Sheila Whiteley, *The Space Between the Notes* (London: Routledge, 1992), 3–4.

67. Susan Fast, *In the Houses of the Holy: Led Zeppelin and the Power of Rock Music* (New York: Oxford University Press, 2001), 36.

NOTES TO CHAPTER THREE

1. Bill Dobbins, *Chick Corea, Piano Improvisations* (Rottenburg: Advance Music, 1991).

2. "Descent into the Maelstrom" is both the name of a Tristano recording made in his home studio in 1953 and a subsequent LP release that packaged the recording along with a number of others. According to Eunmi Shim, Tristano had made some solo sessions for RCA Victor in 1947 but not authorized their release. Eunmi Shim, *Lennie Tristano: His Life in Music* (Ann Arbor: University of Michigan Press, 2007), 42. The Evans recording *Conversations with Myself* employs overdubbing, something that rather distinguishes it from these other records. *Bill Evans Alone* from 1968 is therefore his first solo release recorded without any overdubbing techniques. The Monk album *Thelonious Himself* includes one track on which John Coltrane and Wilbur Ware are featured.

3. Dave Brubeck, liner notes to *Brubeck Plays Brubeck*, Columbia Records, 1956, CL 878.

4. "Interview with Keith Jarrett" http://dothemath.typepad.com/dtm/interview-with-keith-jarrett.html (July 5, 2011). The interview was, as indicated on the webpage, organized by the BBC and broadcast in part on BBC Radio 3 in 2009. The other pianist

Jarrett talks about in this interview as particularly significant in his early listening is Ahmad Jamal.

5. "Descent into the Maelstrom" was Tristano's attempt to portray in sonic terms a story of the same name by Edgar Allan Poe. Shim, *Lennie Tristano*, 87.

6. Barry Ulanov, liner notes to Lennie Tristano, *The New Tristano*, Atlantic 1357, 1962.

7. Andrew Raffo Dewar, "Searching for the Center of a Sound: Bill Dixon's *Webern*, the Unaccompanied Solo, and Compositional Ontology in Post-Songform Jazz," *Jazz Perspectives* 4/1 (2010): 59–87.

8. Radano, *New Musical Figurations*, 131–32.

9. Anthony Braxton, keynote address at the Guelph Jazz Festival, 2007. Reproduced in *Critical Studies in Improvisation* 4/1 (2008) http://www.criticalimprov.com/article/view/520 (October 27, 2010).

10. See for instance Monson, *Freedom Sounds*; Scott Saul, *Freedom Is, Freedom Ain't: Jazz and the Making of the Sixties* (Cambridge, MA: Harvard University Press, 2003).

11. I am grateful to an anonymous reviewer for pointing this out to me.

12. John S. Wilson, "Return of Unaccompanied Pianists," *New York Times* (July 7, 1974): 30.

13. Author unknown, "Newport in New York," *Jazz Podium* (September 1974): 17–18.

14. Jon Balleras, "Paul Bley, *Open, To Love*," *Down Beat* 42/6 (March 27, 1975): 17–18.

15. Klaus Robert Bachmann, "Steve Kuhn und Oregon in Freiburg," *Jazz Podium* (August 1975): 17.

16. At the time of writing, the Kuhn recording has been rereleased as part of an ECM set entitled *Life's Backward Glances* (ECM 2090-92), 2009.

17. Ron Welburn, "The Unaccompanied Jazz Soloist," *Music Journal*, 34/8 (1976): 34.

18. Steve Lake and Paul Griffiths, eds., *Horizons Touched: The Music of ECM* (London: Granta, 2007), 251.

19. Ibid., 226.

20. Michael Ullman, "Starting from Zero: ECM at 25," *Schwann Spectrum* (Fall 1994): 9.

21. "Crystal Silence: The ECM Story," documentary broadcast on BBC Radio 3, May 1996.

22. Robert Hodson, *Interaction, Improvisation and Interplay in Jazz* (New York: Routledge, 2007), 76–77.

23. Barry Kernfeld, *What to Listen for in Jazz* (New Haven: Yale University Press, 1995), 73.

24. Eric Charry, "Freedom and Form in Ornette Coleman's Early Atlantic Recordings," *Annual Review of Jazz Studies* 9 (1997): 261–94.

25. Hodson, *Interaction, Improvisation and Interplay in Jazz*, 115–17.

26. Derek Bailey, *Improvisation, Its Nature and Practice in Music* (London: British Library, 1992), xi.

27. See Keith Waters, *The Studio Recordings of the Miles Davis Quintet, 1965–68* (New York: Oxford University Press, 2011), 76–81.

28. Robert Hodson, "Breaking Down the Barriers: Steps Toward Free Jazz," *IAJE Jazz Research Proceedings Yearbook*, XXX (2000): 102–10.

29. Ekkehard Jost, *Free Jazz* (New York: Da Capo Press, 1994), 9–10.

30. Example 3.1 is adapted from a transcription Simon Savary has made of this piece, released under a Creative Commons license.

31. Example 3.2 is based on an anonymous transcription of this piece that circulates on the internet. I have taken a different rhythmic approach from the original transcriber.

32. David Ake, "Re-Masculating Jazz: Ornette Coleman, 'Lonely Woman,' and the New York Jazz Scene of the Late 1950s," *American Music* 16/1 (Spring 1998): 25–44.

NOTES TO CHAPTER FOUR

1. See Ed Sarath, "A New Look at Improvisation," *Journal of Music Theory* 40/1 (Spring 1996): 1–38.
2. Jost, *Free Jazz*, 14.
3. Gunther Schuller, *Early Jazz* (New York: Oxford University Press, 1968), x.
4. Perhaps the single most important contribution to this idea in recent years is Paul Berliner's book *Thinking in Jazz: The Infinite Art of Improvisation* (Chicago: University of Chicago Press, 1994).
5. For a useful survey of the various theoretical approaches gathered under the umbrella of intertextuality, see Graham Allen, *Intertextuality* (Oxford: Routledge, 2000).
6. Ibid., 66.
7. Evan Eisenberg, *The Recording Angel* (New Haven: Yale University Press, 2005). Serge Lacasse, "Intertextuality and Hypertextuality in Recorded Popular Music," in *The Musical Work: Reality or Invention*, ed. Michael Talbot (Liverpool: Liverpool University Press, 2000), 35–58.
8. Rub, "The Baden Concert."
9. Nicholas Cook, "Music Minus One," *New Formations* 27 (1995): 23–41.
10. Jeff Pressing, "Cognitive Processes in Improvisation," in *Cognitive Processes in the Perception of Art*, eds. Ray Crozier and Anthony Chapman (Amsterdam: Elsevier, 1984), 346.
11. Ibid., 349.
12. Gernot Blume, "Musical Practices and Identity Construction in the Work of Keith Jarrett," Ph.D. diss., University of Michigan, 1998.
13. Bailey, *Improvisation, Its Nature and Practice in Music*, xi.
14. Gernot Blume, "Blurred Affinities: Tracing the Influence of North Indian Classical Music in Keith Jarrett's Solo Piano Improvisations," *Popular Music* 22/2 (2003): 119.
15. Blume, "Musical Practices and Identity Construction," 131–35.
16. See Peter Elsdon, "Style and the Improvised in Keith Jarrett's Solo Concerts," *Jazz Perspectives* 2/1 (May 2008): 51–67.
17. See for instance "Is It Really the Same?" from Charles Lloyd, *Love-In*, Atlantic Records 1481, 1967.
18. Elsdon, "Style and the Improvised."
19. Stephen Termini, "The Art of the Improviser Is the Art of Forgetting: Conspiracies of Freedom and Constraint in the Improvisations of Keith Jarrett," Ph.D. diss., Royal Academy of Music, University of London, 2006, 44–50.
20. Robert Hatten, *Musical Meaning in Beethoven: Markedness, Correlation, and Interpretation* (Bloomington: Indiana University Press, 1994), 67.
21. Richard Williams, "Keith Jarrett," *The Times* (October 24, 1977): 7.
22. John Corbett, *Extended Play* (Durham, NC: Duke University Press, 1994), 222.

23. Thomas Owens, "Charlie Parker: Techniques of Improvisation," Ph.D. diss., University of California at Los Angeles, 1974.

24. Lawrence Gushee, "Lester Young's 'Shoeshine Boy,'" in *Report of the Twelfth Congress, Berkeley 1977*, eds. Daniel Heartz and Bonnie Wade (Kassel: Barenreiter, 1977), 151–69. Gregory Smith, "Homer, Gregory and Bill Evans? The Theory of Formulaic Composition in the Context of Jazz Piano Improvisation," Ph.D. diss., Harvard University, 1983.

25. Corbett, *Extended Play*, 225.

26. Ibid., 224.

27. For more on Schutz and the implications of his work for the study of jazz, see Nicholas Cook, "Making Music Together, or Improvisation and Its Others," *The Source* 1 (2004): 5–26.

28. Vijay Iyer, "Improvisation, Temporality and Embodied Experience," *Journal of Consciousness Studies* 11/3 (2004): 162.

29. Randall Bauer, "A Certain State of Surrender: Toward a Jarrettian Landscape of Spontaneity," Ph.D. diss., Princeton University, 2005, 65.

NOTES TO CHAPTER FIVE

1. See for instance Susan McClary and Robert Walser, "Start Making Sense! Musicology Wrestles with Rock," in *On Record: Rock, Pop and the Written Word*, eds. Simon Frith and Andrew Goodwin (London: Routledge, 1990), 277–92.

2. Berliner, *Thinking in Jazz*, 71–82.

3. Keith Jarrett, *The Köln Concert, Original Transcription* (Mainz: Schott, 1991).

4. Moreno, "Body'n'soul: Keith Jarrett's Pianism."

5. Susan McClary. *Feminine Endings: Music, Gender and Sexuality* (Minneapolis: University of Minnesota Press, 1991), 136.

6. Termini, "The Art of the Improviser," 340.

7. Corinna da Fonseca-Wollheim, "A Jazz Night to Remember," *Wall Street Journal*, October 11, 2008. http://online.wsj.com/article/SB122367103134923957.html (August 10, 2011).

8. Ake, "The Emergence of the Rural American Ideal in Jazz," 29–59.

9. Walter Everett, *The Beatles as Musicians: The Quarry Men Through Rubber Soul* (New York: Oxford University Press, 2001), 360.

10. Blume, "Musical Practices and Identity Construction," 131–35.

11. Termini, "The Art of the Improviser," 284.

12. Ibid., 299.

13. Elsdon, "Style and the Improvised."

14. Alyn Shipton, unpublished interview with Keith Jarrett. Parts of this interview were broadcast on "Jazz File," BBC Radio 3, April 30 and May 7, 14, 21, 2005.

15. Keith Jarrett, liner notes to *Solo Concerts*.

16. Bruno Nettl et al. "Improvisation," in *Grove Music Online*. http://www.oxfordmusiconline.com/subscriber/article/grove/music/13738pg3 (December 15, 2010).

17. Philip Strange, "Keith Jarrett's Up-tempo Jazz Trio Playing: Transcription and Analysis of Performances of 'Just In Time,'" Ph.D. diss., University of Miami, 2003, 141.

18. Termini, "The Art of the Improviser," 61.
19. Ibid., 45.
20. Peter Elsdon, "Keith Jarrett's Solo Concerts and the Aesthetics of Free Improvisation, 1960–1973," Ph.D. diss., University of Southampton, 2001, 197.
21. Whiteley, *The Space Between the Notes*, 3–4. See also Edward Macan, *Rocking the Classics: English Progressive Rock and the Counterculture* (New York: Oxford University Press, 1997), 13.
22. Tia DeNora, *Music in Everyday Life* (Cambridge: Cambridge University Press, 2000), 31.
23. Neil Tesser, "Keith Jarrett: *Sun Bear Concerts*," *Down Beat* 46/4 (February 22, 1979): 24.

NOTES TO CHAPTER SIX

1. The *Dark Intervals* recording of 1987 documents Jarrett playing solo performances comprising short improvised pieces, rather than long improvisations that would each take half of a concert. This was a format Jarrett returned to on the recording *Radiance* from 2005, and which subsequently he seems to have adhered to (further recordings such as *Testament* and *The Carnegie Hall Concert* employ the same format). By and large, though, Jarrett seems to have favored the long-piece format, certainly up to when the *Dark Intervals* recording was made.
2. Barry Kernfeld, "Groove (i)," in *Grove Music Online, Oxford Music Online*. http://www.oxfordmusiconline.com/subscriber/article/grove/music/J582400 (July 14, 2011).
3. Steven Feld, "Aesthetics as Iconicity of Style, or 'Lift-up-over Sounding': Getting into the Kaluli Groove," *Yearbook for Traditional Music*, xx (1988): 74, quoted in Kernfeld, "Groove."
4. Monson, "Saying Something," 68.
5. See for instance Matthew Butterfield, "The Power of Anacrusis; Engendered Feeling in Groove-Based Musics," *Music Theory Online* 4/12 (2006). http://www.mtosmt.org/issues/mto.06.12.4/mto.06.12.4.butterfield.html (August 12, 2011).
6. This footage does not currently seem to be commercially available. However at the time of writing it can be found on a number of internet sites, including YouTube.
7. Elsdon, "Style and the Improvised."
8. Keith Jarrett, *The Köln Concert: Original Transcription* (Mainz: Schott, 1991).
9. Termini identifies smooth voice leading as a key feature of Jarrett's improvisatory approach, or what he calls "automata." Termini, "The Art of the Improviser Is the Art of Forgetting," 44.
10. Ibid., 44–50.
11. More information is at http://www.discogs.com/Keith-Jarrett-Encore-From-The-K%C3%B6ln-Concert-Excerpt/release/2623412 (July 14, 2011).
12. This was pointed out by a poster to the Keith Jarrett group on Yahoo groups.
13. "A Note from 'B', co-author of the Real Book." http://www.personal.psu.edu/bdk4/ (January 12, 2011).
14. Jim Aikin, "Keith Jarrett," *Contemporary Keyboard* (September 1979): 40.
15. This passage has been discussed by a number of writers on Jarrett. See Blume, "Musical Practices and Identity Construction," 139–42; Aikin, "Keith Jarrett," 44–45.

16. One Jarrett discography available online has the piece from the Frankfurt perfor-mance listed as "Song of the Heart," although it is unclear where this title comes from. The TV broadcast of this concert I have seen provides no song titles on screen.

17. In both the Freiburg and Paris concerts, Jarrett departs from this theme after about four minutes. In the Paris concert the theme is reworked through a number of tex-tures and rhythmic feels, quite unlike the Freiburg performance.

18. See for instance Bruno Nettl, "Introduction," in *In the Course of Performance: Studies in the World of Musical Improvisation*, eds. Bruno Nettl and Melinda Russell (Chi-cago: University of Chicago Press, 1998), 9.

19. Bruno Nettl, "Thoughts on Improvisation: A Comparative Approach," *Musical Quar-terly* 60 (1974): 1–19.

20. See for instance Laudan Nooshin, "Improvisation As 'Other': Creativity, Knowledge and Power—the Case of Iranian Classical Music," *Journal of the Royal Musical Asso-ciation* 128/2 (2003): 242–96.

NOTES TO CHAPTER SEVEN

1. See Manfred Eicher's comments in a recent interview with Gary Giddins. Giddins, "A Conversation with Manfred Eicher."

2. Edward Strickland, *American Composers: Dialogues on Contemporary Music* (Bloom-ington: Indiana University Press, 1991), 30.

3. *The New Age* was even the name of a journal published by A. R. Orage, a British writer who was closely associated with G. I. Gurdjieff.

4. Carr, *Keith Jarrett*, 41.

5. Nicholson, *Jazz Rock*, 90. The key text Ouspensky produced, *In Search of the Miracu-lous*, has come to be seen as the most accessible account of Gurdjieff's teachings. P. D. Ouspensky, *In Search of the Miraculous* (London, Penguin: 1987).

6. Carr, *Keith Jarrett*, 48–51.

7. A good (although not perhaps entirely objective) account of the creation of these pieces is provided in the preface to the Schott editions. Linda Daniel-Spitz, Charles Ketcham, and Laurence Rosenthal, *Gurdjieff/De Hartmann, Music for the Piano, Volume III* (Mainz: Schott, 2002).

8. See James Webb, *The Harmonious Circle* (London: Thames and Hudson, 1980), 240–41.

9. Christopher Chase, "Music, Aesthetics and Legitimation: Keith Jarrett and the 'Fourth Way'," unpublished paper presented at 2010 Midwest Popular Culture Association and Midwest American Culture Association Conference, Minneapolis, October 1, 2010.

10. See for instance Paul Heelas, *The New Age Movement* (Oxford: Blackwell, 1996).

11. Charles Lloyd, *Pathless Path*, Unity Records, 1979.

12. David Fricke, "New Age, Old Hat," *Rolling Stone* 228 (December 16, 1976): 95, 98, 100.

13. Bill Evans, *Bill Evans Plays the Theme from the V.I.P.s and Other Great Songs*, MGM E 4184, 1963. Paul Desmond, *Desmond Blue*, RCA Victor LPM 2438, 1961.

14. Fricke, "New Age, Old Hat."

15. Chuck Berg, "The Winds of Folk," *Lawrence Journal World* (March 6, 1983): 5D.

16. Berg, "The Winds of Folk."
17. Neil Tesser, "Pat Metheny: *Watercolors*," *Down Beat* 45/1 (January 12, 1978): 24.
18. Advertisement in *Yoga Journal* (November/December 1980): 53.
19. Small, *Musicking*.
20. Walter Benjamin, "The Work of Art in the Age of Mechanical Reproduction," *Illumi-nations*, ed. Hannah Arendt (London: Fontana, 1973), 219–53.
21. DeNora, *Music in Everyday Life*, 7.
22. Francisco X. Stork, *Marcelo in the Real World* (New York: Arthur A. Levine Books, 2009). http://www.arthuralevinebooks.com/book.asp?bookid=152 (November 29, 2010).
23. Ibid., 144.
24. Jane Elmor, *Pictures of You* (London: Pan Macmillan, 2009).
25. Bertice Berry, *Redemption Song* (London: One World/Ballantine, 2001).
26. Trezza Azzopardi, *The Song House* (London: Picador, 2010), 220.
27. I have found a considerable number of other similar instances, where the record is mentioned fulfilling a role as background music. See for instance Daniel Peters, *Rising from the Ruins* (London: Random House, 1995), 37; and Mary Morris, *The Bus of Dreams* (Boston: Houghton Mifflin, 1985), 173.
28. See the summary on the publisher's website. http://www.routledgementalhealth.com/you-bring-out-the-music-in-me-9780789060389 (July 19, 2011).
29. Louise Lynch, "Music Therapy: Its Historical Relationships and Value in Programs for the Long-Term Care Setting," in *You Bring Out the Music in Me*, ed. D. Rosemary Cassano (London: Routledge, 1996), 5–16.
30. Jean Houston, *The Hero and the Goddess* (Wheaton, IL: Quest Books, 2009), 454–58.

BIBLIOGRAPHY

Aikin, Jim. "Keith Jarrett." *Contemporary Keyboard* (September 1979): 38–54.

Ake, David. "Re-Masculating Jazz: Ornette Coleman, 'Lonely Woman', and the New York Jazz Scene of the Late 1950s." *American Music* 16/1 (Spring 1998): 25–44.

———. *Jazz Cultures*. Los Angeles: University of California Press, 2002.

———. "The Emergence of the Rural American Ideal in Jazz: Keith Jarrett and Pat Metheny on ECM." *Jazz Perspectives* 1/1 (2007): 29–59.

Allen, Graham. *Intertextuality*. Oxford: Routledge, 2000.

Aronoff, Herbert. "Fine Pianist Plays Mystical Music." *Montreal Gazette* (October 24, 1974): 52.

Atkins, E. Taylor, ed. *Jazz Planet*. Jackson: University of Mississippi Press, 2003.

Auslander, Philip. *Liveness: Performance in a Mediatized Culture*. London: Routledge, 1999.

Bailey, Derek. *Improvisation, Its Nature and Practice in Music*. London: British Library, 1992.

Bauer, Randall. "A Certain State of Surrender: Toward a Jarrettian Landscape of Spontaneity." Ph.D. diss., Princeton University, 2005.

Benjamin, Walter. "The Work of Art in the Age of Mechanical Reproduction." In *Illuminations*, ed. Hannah Arendt, 219–53. London: Fontana, 1973.

Berliner, Paul F. *Thinking in Jazz, the Infinite Art of Improvisation*. Chicago: University of Chicago Press, 1994.

Bley, Paul, with David Lee. *Stopping Time: Paul Bley and the Transformation of Jazz*. Montreal, Que., Canada: Vehicule Press, 1999.

Blume, Gernot. "Musical Practices and Identity Construction in the Work of Keith Jarrett." Ph.D. diss., University of Michigan, 1998.

———. "Blurred Affinities: Tracing the Influence of North Indian Classical Music in Keith Jarrett's Solo Piano Improvisations." *Popular Music* 22/2 (2003): 117–42.

Borgo, David. *Sync or Swarm: Improvising Music in a Complex Age*. New York: Continuum, 2005.

Budds, Michael J. *Jazz in the Sixties: The Expansion of Musical Resources and Techniques.* Iowa City: University of Iowa Press, 1990.

Butterfield, Matthew. "Music Analysis and the Social Life of Jazz Recordings." *Current Musicology* 71–73 (Spring 2001–Spring 2002): 324–52.

———. "The Power of Anacrusis: Engendered Feeling in Groove-Based Musics." *Music Theory Online* 4/12 (2006). http://www.mtosmt.org/issues/mto.06.12.4/mto.06.12.4. butterfield.html (August 22, 2011).

Carr, Ian. *Keith Jarrett: The Man and His Music.* London: Paladin, 1992.

Charry, Eric. "Freedom and Form in Ornette Coleman's Early Atlantic Recordings." *Annual Review of Jazz Studies* 9 (1997): 261–94.

Chase, Christopher. "Music, Aesthetics and Legitimation: Keith Jarrett and the 'Fourth Way.'" Unpublished paper presented at 2010 Midwest Popular Culture Association and Midwest American Culture Association Conference, Minneapolis, October 1, 2010.

Clecak, Peter. *America's Quest for the Ideal Self.* New York: Oxford University Press, 1983.

Collier, James Lincoln. "Jazz in the Jarrett Mode." *New York Times* (January 7, 1979): 17.

Conroy, Frank. "Mr. Epiphany." *New Times* (April 1, 1977): 53.

Cook, Nicholas. "Music Minus One." *New Formations* 27 (1995): 23–41.

———. "Between Process and Product: Music and/as Performance." *Music Theory Online* 7/2 (2001): 1–31. http://www.mtosmt.org/issues/mto.01.7.2/mto.01.7.2.cook.html (August 22, 2011).

———. "Making Music Together, or Improvisation and Its Others." *The Source* 1 (2004): 5–26.

Cook, Nicholas, Eric Clarke, Daniel Leech-Wilkinson, and John Rink, eds. *The Cambridge Companion to Recorded Music.* Cambridge: Cambridge University Press, 2009.

Corbett, John. *Extended Play.* Durham: Duke University Press, 1994.

Cottrell, Stephen. "The Rise and Rise of Phonomusicology." In *Recorded Music: Performance, Culture and Technology,* ed. Amanda Bayley, 15–36. Cambridge: Cambridge University Press, 2010.

Cuscuna, Michael. "Strictly on the Record: The Art of Jazz and the Recording Industry." *The Source* 2 (2005): 63–70.

Davidson, Jane W. "Visual Perception of Performance Manner in the Movements of Solo Musicians." *Psychology of Music* 2/1 (1993): 103–13.

Davis, Miles, with Quincy Troupe. *Miles: The Autobiography.* New York: Simon and Schuster, 1989.

Dean, Roger, and Hazel Smith. *Improvisation, Hypermedia and the Arts Since 1945.* Amsterdam: Harwood, 1997.

DeNora, Tia. *Music in Everyday Life.* Cambridge: Cambridge University Press, 2000.

DeVeaux, Scott. "Bebop and the Recording Industry: The 1942 AFM Recording Ban Reconsidered." *Journal of the American Musicological Society* 41/1 (1988): 126–65.

———. "Constructing the Jazz Tradition: Jazz Historiography." *Black American Literature Forum* 25/3 (Autumn 1991): 525–60.

———. *The Birth of Bebop.* Los Angeles: University of California Press, 1998.

Dewar, Andrew Raffo. "Searching for the Center of a Sound: Bill Dixon's *Webern,* the Unaccompanied Solo, and Compositional Ontology in Post-Songform Jazz." *Jazz Perspectives* 4/1 (2010): 59–87.

Dobbins, Bill. *Chick Corea, Piano Improvisations*. Rottenburg, Ger.: Advance Music, 1991.

Eisenberg, Evan. *The Recording Angel*. New Haven: Yale University Press, 2005.

Elsdon, Peter. "Keith Jarrett's Solo Concerts and the Aesthetics of Free Improvisation, 1960–1973." Ph.D. diss., University of Southampton, 2001.

———. "Listening in the Gaze: The Body in Keith Jarrett's Solo Piano Improvisations." In *Music and Gesture*, eds. Elaine King and Anthony Gritten, 192–207. Aldershot: Ashgate, 2006.

———. "Style and the Improvised in Keith Jarrett's Solo Concerts." *Jazz Perspectives* 2/1 (2008): 51–67.

———. "Jazz Recordings and the Capturing of Performance." In *Recorded Music: Performance, Culture and Technology*, edited by Amanda Bayley, 146–63. Cambridge: Cambridge University Press, 2010.

Everett, Walter. *The Beatles as Musicians: The Quarry Men Through Rubber Soul*. New York: Oxford University Press, 2001.

Fast, Susan. *In the Houses of the Holy: Led Zeppelin and the Power of Rock Music*. New York: Oxford University Press, 2001.

Feather, Leonard. "Jarrett: Harbinger of New Forms?" *Los Angeles Times* (June 14, 1976): G19.

Flohr, Karsten. "Jazz-Pianist Begann als Wunderkind." *Hamburger Abendblatt* (January 30, 1975): 9.

———. "Keith Jarrett Vermittelte Zwischen Gestern und Heute." *Hamburger Abendblatt* (February 2, 1975): 23.

Fonseca-Wollheim, Corinna da. "A Jazz Night to Remember." *Wall Street Journal* (October 11, 2008). http://online.wsj.com/article/SB122367103134923957.html (August 10, 2011).

Fordham, John. "50 Great Moments in Jazz: Anthony Braxton Swims Against the Tide." http://www.guardian.co.uk/music/musicblog/2011/apr/13/50-moments-anthony-braxton-jazz (July 5, 2011).

———. "50 Great Moments in Jazz: Keith Jarrett's The Köln Concert." http://www.guardian.co.uk/music/musicblog/2011/jan/31/50-great-moments-jazz-keith-jarrett (July 5, 2011).

Gennari, John. "Jazz Criticism: Its Development and Ideologies." *Black American Literature Forum* 25/3 (1991): 449–523.

———. *Blowin' Hot and Cool: Jazz and Its Critics*. Chicago: University of Chicago Press, 2006.

Gracyk, Theodore. *Rhythm and Noise: An Aesthetics of Rock*. London: Tauris, 1996.

Graebner, William. "America's Poseidon Adventure: A Nation in Existential Despair." In *America in the 70s*, eds. Beth Bailey and David Farber, 157–80. Lawrence: University Press of Kansas, 2004.

Gushee, Lawrence. "Lester Young's 'Shoeshine Boy.'" In *Report of the Twelfth Congress, Berkeley 1977*, edited by Daniel Heartz and Bonnie Wade, 151–69. Kassel: Barenreiter, 1977.

Hatten, Robert. *Musical Meaning in Beethoven: Markedness, Correlation, and Interpretation*. Bloomington: Indiana University Press, 1994.

Heelas, Paul. *The New Age Movement*. Oxford: Blackwell, 1996.

Heffley, Mike. *Northern Sun, Southern Moon: Europe's Reinvention of Jazz*. New Haven: Yale University Press, 2005.

Hodson, Robert. "Breaking Down the Barriers: Steps Toward Free Jazz." *IAJE Jazz Research Proceedings Yearbook*, XXX (2000): 102–10.

——— . *Interaction, Improvisation, and Interplay in Jazz*. New York: Routledge, 2007.

Hurley, Andrew Wright. *The Return of Jazz: Joachim-Ernst Berendt and West German Cultural Change*. New York: Berghahn, 2009.

Iyer, Vijay. "Embodied Mind, Situated Cognition, and Expressive Microtiming in African-American Music." *Music Perception* 19/3 (2002): 387–414.

——— . "Improvisation, Temporality and Embodied Experience." *Journal of Consciousness Studies* 11/3 (2004): 159–73.

Jarrett, Keith. *The Köln Concert: Original Transcription*. Mainz: Schott, 1991.

Johnson, Bruce. "The Jazz Diaspora." In *The Cambridge Companion to Jazz*, eds. Mervyn Cooke and David Horn, 33–54. Cambridge: Cambridge University Press, 2002.

Jost, Ekkehard. *Free Jazz*. New York: Da Capo Press, 1994.

Kernfeld, Barry. *What to Listen for in Jazz*. New Haven: Yale University Press, 1995.

——— . "Pop Song Piracy, Fake Books, and a Pre-History of Sampling." Paper delivered at *Copyright and the Networked Computer*. University of California Washington Center, Washington, DC, 2003. http://www.personal.psu.edu/bdk4/PREHISTORY.pdf (August 22, 2011).

——— . "Groove (i)." In *Grove Music Online, Oxford Music Online*. http://www.oxfordmusiconline.com/subscriber/article/grove/music/J582400 (July 14, 2011).

Klee, Joe. "Keith Jarrett, Spontaneous Composer." *Down Beat* 39/1 (January 20, 1972): 12, 36.

Lacasse, Serge. "Intertextuality and Hypertextuality in Recorded Popular Music." In *The Musical Work: Reality or Invention*, ed. Michael Talbot, 35–58. Liverpool: Liverpool University Press, 2000.

Lake, Steve. "Jarrett: Romance Is Not Dead." *Melody Maker* (December 11, 1975): 43.

——— , and Paul Griffiths, eds. *Horizons Touched: The Music of ECM*. London: Granta, 2007.

Laverne, Andy. "Inside Keith Jarrett's 'In Front.'" *Keyboard Magazine* (March 1988): 112–13.

Lewis, George. "Improvised Music After 1950: Afrological and Eurological Perspectives." In *The Other Side of Nowhere*, eds. Daniel Fischlin and Ajay Heble, 131–62. Middletown, CT: Wesleyan University Press, 2004.

——— . *A Power Stronger Than Itself: The AACM and American Experimental Music*. Chicago: University of Chicago Press, 2008.

Luty, Bryce. "Jazz Ensembles' Era of Accelerated Growth, Part II." *Music Educators Journal* 69/4 (1982): 49–50, 64.

Macan, Edward. *Rocking the Classics: English Progressive Rock and the Counterculture*. New York: Oxford University Press, 1997.

Malson, Lucien. "Jazz: Keith Jarrett." *Le Monde* (February 7, 1975): 28.

McClary, Susan. *Feminine Endings: Music, Gender and Sexuality*. Minneapolis: University of Minnesota Press, 1991.

——— , and Robert Walser. "Start Making Sense! Musicology Wrestles with Rock." In *On Record: Rock, Pop and the Written Word*, eds. Simon Frith and Andrew Goodwin, 277–92. London: Routledge, 1990.

Mikowksi, Bill. "Jarrett Is Mix of Lunatic, Genius." *Milwaukee Journal* (November 19, 1977): 7.

Mimaroglu, Ilhan. "Keith Jarrett, Mercer Arts Center, New York City." *Down Beat* 40/1 (January 18, 1973): 36.

Monson, Ingrid. *Saying Something: Jazz Improvisation and Interaction*. Chicago: University of Chicago Press, 1996.

——— . *Freedom Sounds: Civil Rights Call out to Jazz and Africa*. New York: Oxford University Press, 2007.

Moreno, Jairo. "Body'n'soul: Keith Jarrett's Pianism." *Musical Quarterly* 83/1 (Spring 1999): 75–92.

Nettl, Bruno. "Thoughts on Improvisation: A Comparative Approach." *Musical Quarterly* 60 (1974): 1–19.

——— , and Melinda Russell, eds. *In the Course of Performance: Studies in the World of Musical Improvisation*. Chicago: University of Chicago Press, 1998.

Nettl, Bruno, and Gabriel Soli, eds. *Musical Improvisation: Art, Education, and Society*. Urbana: University of Illinois Press, 2009.

Nettl, Bruno, et al. "Improvisation." In *Grove Music Online, Oxford Music Online*. http://www.oxfordmusiconline.com/subscriber/article/grove/music/13738pg3 (December 15, 2010).

Nicholson, Stuart. *Jazz Rock: A History*. Edinburgh: Canongate, 1998.

Nooshin, Laudan. "Improvisation As 'Other': Creativity, Knowledge and Power—the Case of Iranian Classical Music." *Journal of the Royal Musical Association* 128/2 (2003): 242–96.

Ouspensky, P. D. *In Search of the Miraculous*. London, Penguin: 1987.

Owens, Thomas. "Charlie Parker: Techniques of Improvisation." Ph.D. diss., University of California at Los Angeles, 1974.

Palmer, Bob. "Keith Jarrett, *Facing You*." *Rolling Stone* 124 (December 21, 1972): 48.

——— . "The Inner Octaves of Keith Jarrett." *Down Beat* 41/17 (October 24, 1974): 16–17, 46.

——— . "Keith Jarrett: *Luminescence*." *Rolling Stone* 200 (November 20, 1975): 68, 71.

Panken, Ted. "What Am I Doing?" *Down Beat* 75/12 (December 2008): 37.

Porter, Eric. *What Is This Thing Called Jazz?* Los Angeles: University of California Press, 2002.

——— . "Introduction: Rethinking Jazz Through the 1970s." *Jazz Perspectives* 4/1 (2010): 1–5.

Porter, Lewis. "John Coltrane's *A Love Supreme*: Jazz Improvisation as Composition." *Journal of the American Musicological Society* 38/3 (1985): 593–621.

——— . *Jazz: A Century of Change*. New York: Schirmer, 1998.

Pressing, Jeff. "Cognitive Processes in Improvisation." In *Cognitive Processes in the Perception of Art*, eds. Ray Crozier and Anthony Chapman, 345–63. Amsterdam: Elsevier, 1984.

Radano, Ronald. *New Musical Figurations: Anthony Braxton's Cultural Critique*. Chicago: University of Chicago Press, 1993.

Ramshaw, Sara. "Deconstructin(g) Jazz Improvisation: Derrida and the Law of the Singular Event." *Critical Studies in Improvisation* 2/1 (2006). http://www.criticalimprov.com/article/view/81 (August 22, 2011).

Rasula, Jed. "The Media of Memory: The Seductive Menace of Records in Jazz History." In *Jazz Among the Discourses*, ed. Krin Gabbard, 134–62. London: Duke University Press, 1995.

Ratner, Leonard. *Classic Music*. New York: Schirmer, 1980.

Reich, Charles. *The Greening of America*. New York: Random House, 1970.

Roberts, J. S. "In the Middle with Jarrett." *Melody Maker* (April 12, 1975): 40.

Rodriguez, Juan. "Jarrett Treats Fans to a Philosophy of Music." *Montreal Gazette* (August 30, 1979): 25.

Roszak, Theodore. *The Making of a Counterculture*. London: Faber and Faber, 1970.

Rub, Bruno. "The Baden Concert. Keith Jarrett's Badener Gastspiel am Tag nach dem legendären 'Köln Concert'." *Badener Neujahrsblätter* 2006 (2006): 150–56.

Sarath, Ed. "A New Look at Improvisation." *Journal of Music Theory* 40/1 (Spring 1996): 1–38.

Saul, Scott. *Freedom Is, Freedom Ain't: Jazz and the Making of the Sixties*. Cambridge, MA: Harvard University Press, 2003.

Schuller, Gunther. *Early Jazz*. New York: Oxford University Press, 1968.

Schulman, Bruce J. *The Seventies: The Great Shift in American Culture, Society and Politics*. New York: Da Capo Press, 2001.

Shim, Eunmi. *Lennie Tristano: His Life in Music*. Ann Arbor: University of Michigan Press, 2007.

Small, Christopher. *Musicking: The Meanings of Performing and Listening*. Hanover, NH: Wesleyan University Press, University Press of New England, 1998.

Smith, Gregory. "Homer, Gregory and Bill Evans? The Theory of Formulaic Composition in the Context of Jazz Piano Improvisation." Ph.D. diss., Harvard University, 1983.

Solis, Gabriel. *Monk's Music: Thelonious Monk and Jazz History in the Making*. Berkeley and Los Angeles: University of California Press, 2008.

Stockdale, Jonty. "Reading Around Free Improvisation." *The Source* 1 (2004): 101–14.

Strange, Philip. "Keith Jarrett's Up-tempo Jazz Trio Playing: Transcription and Analysis of Performances of 'Just In Time'." Ph.D. diss., University of Miami, 2003.

Strickland, Edward. *American Composers: Dialogues on Contemporary Music*. Bloomington: Indiana University Press, 1991.

Such, David. *Avant-Garde Jazz Musicians: Performing 'Out There'*. Iowa City: University of Iowa Press, 1993.

Sudnow, David. *Ways of the Hand: The Organisation of Improvised Conduct*. Cambridge, MA: MIT Press, 1978.

Székely, Michael David. "Thresholds: Jazz, Improvisation, Heterogeneity, and Politics in Postmodernity." *Jazz Perspectives* 2/1 (2008): 29–50.

Tackley, Catherine. "Jazz Recordings as Social Texts." In *Recorded Music: Performance, Culture, and Technology*, ed. Amanda Bayley, 167–86. Cambridge: Cambridge University Press, 2010.

Termini, Stephen. "The Art of the Improviser Is the Art of Forgetting: Conspiracies of Freedom and Constraint in the Improvisations of Keith Jarrett." Ph.D. diss., Royal Academy of Music, University of London, 2006.

Tesser, Neil. "Keith Jarrett: *The Köln Concert*." *Down Beat* 42/4 (February 12, 1975): 22.

———. "Keith Jarrett: *Sun Bear Concerts*." *Down Beat* 46/4 (February 22, 1979): 24.

Tomlinson, Gary. "Cultural Dialogics and Jazz: A White Historian Signifies." *Black Music Research Journal* 11/12 (Autumn 1991): 229–64.

Ullman, Michael. "Starting from Zero: ECM at 25." *Schwann Spectrum* (Fall 1994): 9.

Walser, Robert. "The Body in the Music: Epistemology and Musical Semiotics." *College Music Symposium* 31 (1991): 117–25.

———, and Susan McClary. "Theorizing the Body in African-American Music." *Black Music Research Journal* 14/1 (Spring 1994): 75–84.

Waters, Keith. *The Studio Recordings of the Miles Davis Quintet, 1965–68.* New York: Oxford University Press, 2011.

Webb, James. *The Harmonious Circle.* London: Thames and Hudson, 1980.

Welburn, Ron. "The Unaccompanied Jazz Soloist." *Music Journal* 34/8 (1976): 34.

Whiteley, Sheila. *The Space Between the Notes.* London: Routledge, 1992.

Whyton, Tony. *Jazz Icons: Heroes, Myths, and the Jazz Tradition.* Cambridge: Cambridge University Press, 2010.

Williams, Richard. "Keith Jarrett." *The Times* (October 24, 1977): 7.

Wilmer, Valerie. *As Serious as Your Life.* London: Serpent's Tail, 1977.

Wilson, John S. "In Dancing Spirits: Jarrett Improvises on the Keyboard." *New York Times* (March 4, 1975): 41.

———. "Jazz Pianist to Slow Pace." *New York Times* (March 23, 1975): 80.

———. "In League with the Jazz Giants." *New York Times* (September 28, 1975): 399.

Wolfe, Tom. *The Purple Decades.* London: Picador, 1993.

DISCOGRAPHY

Beirach, Richard. *Hubris* (ECM 1104), 1978.

Bley, Paul. *Open, To Love* (ECM 1023), 1972.

Brand, Dollar. *African Piano* (ECM 3602), 1969.

Braxton, Anthony. *For Alto* (Delmark DS-420/421), 1971.

Brubeck, Dave. *Brubeck Plays Brubeck* (Columbia Records CL 878), 1956.

Burton, Gary, and Keith Jarrett. *Gary Burton with Keith Jarrett* (Atlantic SD 2577), 1970.

Byard, Jaki. *Blues for Smoke* (Candid CCD 79018), 1960.

Coleman, Ornette. *The Shape of Jazz to Come* (Atlantic 1317), 1959.

Coltrane, John. *Ascension* (Impulse ASD 9228), 1965.

———. *Interstellar Space* (Impulse ASD 9277), 1967.

Corea, Chick. *Piano Improvisations, Vol. 1* (ECM 1014), 1971.

———. *Piano Improvisations, Vol. 2* (ECM 1020), 1971.

Davis, Miles. *Kind of Blue* (Columbia CL 1355), 1959.

———. *My Funny Valentine* (Columbia CS 2306), 1965.

Evans, Bill. *Conversations with Myself* (Verve V/V6 8526), 1963.

Guiffre, Jimmy. *Freefall* (Columbia CB 741), 1963.

Hill, Andrew. *Hommage* (East Wind EW 8017), 1975.

Jarrett, Keith. *Life Between the Exit Signs* (Vortex 2006), 1967.

———. *Restoration Ruin* (Vortex 2008), 1968.

———. *Somewhere Before* (Vortex LP 2012), 1968.

———. *Expectations* (Columbia KG 31580), 1971.

———. *Facing You* (ECM 1017), 1971.

———. *Solo Concerts* (ECM 1035/37), 1973.

———. *Belonging* (ECM 1050), 1974.

———. *Treasure Island* (Impulse AS 9274), 1974.

———. *Backhand* (Impulse AS 9305), 1975.

———. *The Köln Concert* (ECM 1064/65), 1975.

——— . *Hymns/Spheres* (ECM 1086/87), 1976.
——— . *Sun Bear Concerts* (ECM 1100), 1976.
——— . *The Survivor's Suite* (ECM 1085), 1976.
——— . *Byablue* (Impulse AS 9331), 1977.
——— . *Vermont Solo* (VideoArts Music/Cavelight Corporation), 1977.
——— . *G. I. Gurdjieff Sacred Hymns* (ECM 1174), 1980.
——— . *Dark Intervals* (ECM 1379), 1987.
——— . *Last Solo* (VideoArts Music), 1987.
——— . *Keith Jarrett at the Blue Note, the Complete Recordings* (ECM 1575/80), 1994.
——— . *La Scala* (ECM 1640), 1997.
——— . *Radiance* (ECM 1960/61), 2005.
——— . *Carnegie Hall Concert* (ECM 1989/90), 2006.
——— , and Jack DeJohnette. *Ruta and Daitya* (ECM 1021), 1971.
Kühn, Joachim. *Piano Solo* (MSP/BASF 21 21330-7), 1972.
Kuhn, Steve. *Ecstasy* (ECM 1058), 1975.
Lloyd, Charles. *Love-In* (Atlantic 2435), 1967.
McPartland, Marian. *Solo Concert at Haverford* (Halcyon HAL 111), 1974.
Monk, Thelonious. *Thelonious Himself* (Riverside RLP 12-235), 1957.
Rollins, Sonny. *Sonny Meets Hawk* (RCA Victor LPM/LSP-2712), 1963.
Rowles, Jimmy. *Jazz Is a Fleeting Moment* (Jazzz LP 103), 1976.
Towner, Ralph. *Diary* (ECM 1032), 1974.
——— , and Moore, Glen. *Trios/Solos* (ECM 1025), 1973.
Tristano, Lennie. *The New Tristano* (Atlantic LP 1537), 1961.
——— . *Descent into the Maelstrom* (East Wind EW 8040), 1978.
Williams, Mary Lou. *Solo Recital* (Fantasy OJCCD-962-2), 1978.
Winston, George. *Autumn* (Windham Hill Records, WHS C-1012), 1980.

INDEX

Note: sub-chapter heading pages ranges are given in bold type.

Made in the USA
Middletown, DE
12 March 2017